Country Living

Picnics
and
Porch Suppers

Country Living

PICNICS AND PORCH SUPPERS

Text By
DIANA GOLD MURPHY

Foreword By
RACHEL NEWMAN

HEARST BOOKS
NEW YORK · NEW YORK

Library of Congress Cataloging-in-Publication Data is available upon request.

Printed in Singapore
First Edition
1 2 3 4 5 6 7 8 9 10

Country Living Staff
Rachel Newman, Editor-in-Chief
Nancy Mernit Soriano, Editor
Julio Vega, Art Director
John Mack Carter, President, Hearst Magazine Enterprises

www.williammorrow.com

Produced by Smallwood & Stewart, Inc., New York City
Edited by Sarah Stewart
Designed by Anne Scatto / PIXEL PRESS

CONTENTS

FOREWORD

Dining alfresco is one of life's simplest and yet most joyous pleasures. I remember as a child being filled with excitement at the prospect of a picnic— whether it was to celebrate the Fourth of July or just a sunny summer's day. As an adult I find myself eagerly anticipating those occasions spent with friends over an outdoor meal. The aromas and flavors of all food seem to be enhanced by being in the wonderful outdoors.

Over the years the editors at *Country Living* have often encouraged readers to experience the wonder of the great outdoors by bringing meals out into it. Too often, however, people become intimidated by the notion of preparing food for picnics. But when we are armed with some foolproof recipes and basic planning tips, picnicking can be easy and wonderfully rewarding. And the joys of a summer picnic can be experienced year-round by dining on the porch.

The versatility and sheer pleasure of eating outdoors inspired us to offer this latest book, *Country Living Picnics and Porch Suppers*. Packed with great-tasting recipes, creative serving ideas, and practical tips on food storage and transportation, it will inspire even the most devout homebody to pack a hamper and set out in search of the perfect pastorial setting.

Rachel Newman
Editor-in-Chief

INTRODUCTION

The pleasures of dining outdoors are limitless, and can be enjoyed any time of the day or night. Whether it's an impromptu breakfast picnic for two or an elaborate porch supper for a crowd, there's something magical about languishing in the fresh air while feasting on a homemade repast.

Any occasion is cause for celebration, but sometimes life's most precious moments occur when we celebrate day-to-day occurrences: the first warm day of spring, a child's good report card, visits from out-of-town friends, or just because we feel festive. It's especially important these days when we're all so busy to take time out from our hectic schedules to relax and regroup. There's no better way to accomplish this than sitting down to a great meal amid the soft rustle leaves as the breeze sneaks past, being keenly aware of the flutter of butterflies winging between blossoms, the steady chirp of crickets hiding in the grass, and the seemingly endless ceiling of sky that stretches beyond our imagination.

Keep a supply of baskets in all sizes, small ones can stow stemware and napkins while in large ones you can arrange piles of sandwiches, cookies, or breads. Pretty tablecloths, colorful cloth napkins and dish towels are perfect for lining baskets as well as setting the table. Forays into flea markets are a good way to find these plus other essentials such as lanterns, serving platters, and linens.

Picnicking is meant to be fun and the possibilities are endless. From simple last-minute meals, to large formal garden parties`1, just being together with family and friends, enjoying the outdoors, laughing and talking over an excellent meal is what's most important.

BREAKFASTS & BRUNCHES

The early moments of a fine morning are meant to be spent outdoors, where you can dine amidst the awakening of the day, employing all your senses. Whether picnicking or gathering on the porch, take a moment to feel the cool breeze as the morning dew evaporates, capture the fragrance and beauty of the garden, revel in the birdsong, and enjoy the flavors of home cooking. These are life's finest pleasures; there's no better way to start the day.

Raspberry Streusel Muffins

Crumbly streusel topping on tender raspberry-studded muffins will keep guests coming back for more, so you may want to prepare a double batch. Line them in a single layer on a floral serving platter to avoid smudging the confectioners' sugar. For a romantic Valentine's Day brunch, bake the batter in heart-shaped muffin-pan cups.

MAKES 12 MUFFINS

Streusel Topping

½ cup unsifted all-purpose flour

½ cup quick rolled oats

⅓ cup granulated sugar

½ teaspoon ground cinnamon

⅛ teaspoon salt

6 tablespoons (¾ stick) butter

Raspberry Muffins

½ cup (1 stick) butter, softened

½ cup granulated sugar

1 large egg

2 cups unsifted all-purpose flour

½ teaspoon baking powder

½ teaspoon baking soda

½ teaspoon ground cinnamon

¼ teaspoon salt

½ cup milk

½ cup sour cream

1 teaspoon vanilla extract

1 cup fresh raspberries or drained, thawed
    frozen raspberries

Confectioners' sugar

◆ Prepare the streusel topping: In a medium-size bowl, combine the flour, oats, granulated sugar, cinnamon, and salt. With a pastry blender or 2 knives, cut in 6 tablespoons of the butter until the mixture resembles coarse crumbs. Briefly rub the mixture between your fingers to blend in the butter. Set the topping aside.

◆ Prepare the raspberry muffins: Grease twelve 3-inch heart-shaped muffin-pan cups or twelve 3-inch muffin-pan cups. Heat the oven to 400°F.

◆ In a large bowl, with an electric mixer on medium-high speed, beat together the butter and granulated sugar until it is light and fluffy. Add the egg and beat until the mixture is well blended.

◆ In a medium-size bowl, combine the flour, baking powder, baking soda, cinnamon, and salt. In a small bowl, combine the milk, sour cream, and vanilla. Add the flour mixture to the butter mixture alternately with the milk mixture, beating just until the batter is combined. Gently fold in the raspberries.

◆ Spoon the batter into the greased muffin-pan cups, filling each about two-thirds full. Sprinkle the tops of the muffins generously with the streusel topping.

◆ Bake the muffins for 20 to 25 minutes, or until a cake tester inserted in the center comes out clean. Cool the muffins in the pans on wire racks for 5 minutes. Remove the muffins from the cups. Sprinkle the muffins with the confectioners' sugar and serve.

Banana-Date-Nut Muffins

Oat bran adds a healthy dose of fiber to these fruity muffins that will draw everyone to the kitchen as the scent of cinnamon and bananas permeates the house. These baked breakfast treats are a great way to use up over-ripe bananas; the browner the skin, the sweeter the flavor.

MAKES 8 MUFFINS

1¼ cups oat bran

1 cup unsifted all-purpose flour

1 tablespoon baking powder

¼ teaspoon ground cinnamon

¾ cup skim milk

¼ cup light olive, canola, or rice-bran oil

1 tablespoon honey

2 large egg whites or 1 large egg

¾ cup coarsely chopped bananas

⅓ cup pitted dates, chopped

¼ cup walnuts, chopped

◆   Heat the oven to 400°F. Grease eight 2½-inch muffin-pan cups.

◆   In a large bowl, combine the oat bran, flour, baking powder, and cinnamon. In a 2-cup measuring cup or small bowl, stir together the milk, oil, honey, and egg whites.

◆   Add the milk mixture to the flour mixture and stir just until the dry ingredients are completely moistened. Fold in the bananas and dates.

◆   Spoon the batter into the greased muffin-pan cups to fill the cups ⅔ full. Sprinkle the tops of the muffins with the walnuts.

◆   Bake the muffins for 15 to 20 minutes, or until they are golden and the centers spring back when lightly pressed with a fingertip. Cool the muffins in the pan on a wire rack for 5 minutes. Remove the muffins from the cups and serve warm. For a picnic, wrap the warm muffins in aluminum foil. Place the wrapped muffins in a napkin-lined basket. Once at the picnic, unwrap the muffins and arrange in the basket.

◆ FRESH & FRUITY ◆

Of all baked goods, muffins are the most obliging when it comes to your creative whims. All sorts of fruit can be added to muffin batters, whatever is on hand or in season. Use fresh or frozen blueberries, raspberries, blackberries, cranberries, and strawberries interchangeably.

Coarsely chopped chunks of apples, pears, peaches, or plums add subtle sweetness, as do a number of dried fruits such as dates, apricots, raisins, currants, and cherries. Mix and match with your favorite nuts and seeds (poppy, sesame, sunflower) for endless muffin variations.

Apple Breakfast Bread

This light, moist cake is low in fat since applesauce replaces the oil, butter, and egg yolks normally used. Apple slices form a decorative pattern across the top of the quick bread. Fan slices of the bread in an overlapping circle on a round plate, and mound a pile of strawberries in the center before setting out on the porch. For picnics, keep the loaf whole and bring along a serrated knife and cutting board that will double as a serving platter so guests can cut their own slice. In either case, dust with confectioners' sugar just before serving.

MAKES 10 SERVINGS

2 cups unsifted all-purpose flour

½ cup quick rolled oats

1 teaspoon ground cinnamon

1 teaspoon baking soda

½ teaspoon salt

5 large egg whites

¾ cup firmly packed light-brown sugar

1 cup unsweetened applesauce

⅓ cup buttermilk

1 teaspoon vanilla extract

1 Rome Beauty or other red baking apple

Confectioners' sugar

◆ Grease a 12- by 4½-inch loaf pan (or an 8-inch-square baking pan). In a medium-size bowl, combine the flour, oats, cinnamon, baking soda, and salt. Set the flour and oat mixture aside.

◆ Heat the oven to 325°F. In a large bowl, with an electric mixer on medium speed, beat the egg whites with the brown sugar for 2 minutes. Stir in the applesauce until the mixture is well combined. Mix the buttermilk and vanilla and add to the egg-white mixture alternately with the flour mixture, mixing just until combined. Transfer the batter to the greased pan, spreading it evenly.

◆ Quarter and core the apple and cut each quarter lengthwise into 5 slices. Arrange the slices, ⅛ inch apart, peel side up, in a row on top of the bread batter. Bake the bread for 55 to 65 minutes, or until a cake tester inserted in the center comes out clean.

◆ Cool the bread in the pan for 10 minutes. Turn the bread out of the pan and place it right-side up on a wire rack. Cool the bread completely before slicing, and sprinkle it with the confectioners' sugar before serving. For picnics, cool the bread completely and wrap tightly in plastic wrap. Place the confectioners' sugar in a food-storage bag, and prior to serving, sprinkle the bread with the confectioners' sugar.

Baked Eggs with Asparagus

Fresh spring asparagus turns an ordinary egg dish into an elegant brunch. For those watching their waistlines, we've replaced the heavy cream usually called for with skim milk. To keep it warm for picnics, tightly wrap the dish with heavy-duty aluminum foil and nestle it in a towel-lined basket.

MAKES 6 SERVINGS

12 thin stalks (½ pound) asparagus

1 green onion, sliced crosswise

1 teaspoon butter

2 cups skim milk

3 tablespoons all-purpose flour

¼ teaspoon salt

¼ teaspoon cracked black pepper

12 large eggs

Paprika

Fresh herb sprigs such as basil and oregano

◆ Trim off and discard the tough stem ends of the asparagus. In a 3-quart saucepan, heat the asparagus and water to cover to boiling over high heat. Reduce the heat to medium and cook for 1 minute. Drain the asparagus in a colander and set aside.

◆ Heat the oven to 325°F. Lightly grease a 12-inch quiche dish or shallow round baking dish.

◆ In a 1-quart saucepan, sauté the green onion in the butter over medium heat until lightly browned. Stir in 1¾ cups of the milk and heat to boiling. In a 1-cup measuring cup, stir the flour into the remaining ¼ cup milk. Stir the flour mixture into the onion-milk mixture and cook, stirring constantly, until boiling and a thickened sauce forms. Remove the sauce from the heat and set aside.

◆ Cut the asparagus stalks to 4½-inch-long spears; reserve the trimmings. Slice the reserved trimmings crosswise into ¼-inch pieces and stir into the sauce along with the salt and pepper. Pour the sauce into the greased dish. Arrange the asparagus spears on the sauce, spoke fashion, with the tips toward the outside of the dish and the cut ends toward the center.

◆ With a spoon, make a deep hollow in the center of the sauce to hold the excess egg white. Centered between the asparagus spears and about 1 inch in from the edge of the dish, make shallow hollows in the sauce to hold the egg yolks. Crack one egg into each hollow between the asparagus spears so that the yolk rests in the hollow. If necessary, using a spoon, help guide the excess egg white into the hollow in the center of the dish, avoiding touching the yolks.

◆ Carefully place the dish in the oven and bake for 20 to 25 minutes, or until the egg whites are completely set. Sprinkle the top with the paprika and garnish with the herbs sprigs.

Vegetable Frittata

When planning on traveling with a frittata, while it is still in the pan, invert it onto a plate, remove the pan, and place the frittata right-side up on a serving dish. Wrap it tightly in aluminum foil to keep it warm until ready to serve, or slice for sandwiches. Feel free to experiment with this dish by substituting your favorite herbs and vegetables, or adding a handful of grated cheese. This recipe makes individual servings, so you can custom-make each one.

MAKES 1 SERVING

3 large egg whites

1 large egg

2 tablespoons finely chopped fresh chives

⅛ teaspoon salt

⅛ teaspoon ground black pepper

1 spray of nonstick vegetable cooking spray
　　or ¼ teaspoon vegetable oil

½ cup cubed red-skinned potatoes

½ cup broccoli flowerettes

¼ cup coarsely chopped sweet red pepper

⅓ cup water

½ teaspoon vegetable oil

Fresh chives, for garnish

◆ In a medium-size bowl, beat together the egg whites, egg, chopped chives, salt, and pepper until well combined. Set the egg mixture aside.

◆ Heat a 6-, 7-, or 8-inch oven-proof skillet. Lightly coat the skillet with the nonstick vegetable cooking spray. Add the potatoes and sauté them until they are lightly browned. Add the broccoli, red pepper, and water. Cover and cook until the potatoes are fork-tender—3 to 4 minutes. Remove the lid from the skillet and cook the vegetables until the liquid has evaporated.

◆ Stir the ½ teaspoon oil into the vegetables until they are coated.

◆ Add the egg mixture to the skillet. Let the bottom of the egg mixture set, then stir the mixture well. Cover the skillet and continue to cook the eggs until set but still moist on top—about 2 minutes.

◆ Heat the broiler. Uncover the skillet and place the frittata under the broiler, 4 inches from the heat source, and broil until it is browned on top. Garnish with the fresh chives. Serve either hot or at room temperature.

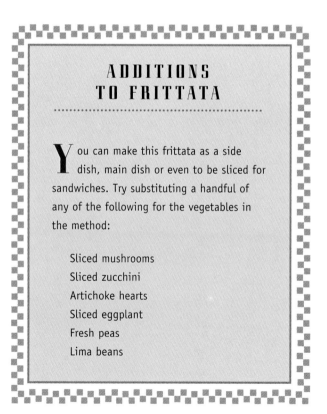

ADDITIONS TO FRITTATA

You can make this frittata as a side dish, main dish or even to be sliced for sandwiches. Try substituting a handful of any of the following for the vegetables in the method:

Sliced mushrooms
Sliced zucchini
Artichoke hearts
Sliced eggplant
Fresh peas
Lima beans

PLANNING
THE FUNDAMENTALS
OF A PICNIC

When you are planning the perfect picnic, keep these tips in mind. When guests are invited in advance, have an alternative plan indoors in case the weather does not comply. Survey the area you plan to dine at beforehand. If you are laying the picnic out on a blanket, look for a spot with level ground, free of tree roots and holes. Check if there are grills available so you are prepared with charcoal, a grill lighter, and grilling utensils. Depending on the type of picnic you plan to have, check the area for necessities. If you are having a fishing picnic, are there boats to rent or a place to launch your boat? It is a good idea to keep your picnic near water for quick and easy clean-up.

Have all your essentials picked out and ready to go the night before. Freeze water to take, pack toys for your children and a water bowl for your animals, and write out a list of the food you'll bring.

Once you get to the picnic site, brush away all debris like twigs and stones before spreading out your blanket. Sit near trees so you have some shade, and if children or animals will be joining you, pick a spot where you can see the surrounding area.

Buttermilk Flapjacks

Easily doubled or tripled for a crowd, flapjacks are fun to make when there are kids around; let them add all their favorites—any kind of berries, sliced bananas, raisins, and chopped apples or pears. Simply mix them into the batter before cooking.

MAKES 3 SERVINGS

2 cups unsifted all-purpose flour

1 tablespoon sugar

½ teaspoon salt

2¼ cups buttermilk

1½ teaspoons baking soda

2 large eggs, lightly beaten

2 tablespoons butter, melted

Vegetable oil, for frying

Butter or margarine

Maple syrup

Fresh strawberries and blueberries
    (optional)

◆ In a large bowl, combine the flour, sugar, and salt. In a small bowl or a glass measuring cup, combine the buttermilk and baking soda. Immediately add the buttermilk mixture, eggs, and melted butter to the flour mixture. Stir just until the dry ingredients are moistened. (The mixture should be lumpy.)

◆ Lightly oil a griddle or 8-inch skillet and heat over medium heat. Spread a heaping ½ cup of the batter onto the griddle to make a 6-inch flapjack. Cook the flapjack until bubbles form and begin to break on the top surface. Turn the flapjack over and cook until the bottom is golden brown. Remove the flapjack and place it on a baking sheet or oven-proof platter in a 200°F oven to keep warm until all the flapjacks are cooked.

◆ Repeat with the remaining batter, adding more oil to the pan as necessary. Serve the flapjacks warm, with butter and maple syrup, and strawberries and blueberries, if desired.

Sweet-Cherry Pancakes

Cornmeal and sweet cherries give these pancakes a toasty, sweet flavor. If cherries aren't in season, substitute fresh blueberries, raspberries, strawberries, or sliced bananas.

MAKES 6 PANCAKES

1¼ cups unsifted all-purpose flour

¾ cup yellow cornmeal

2 tablespoons sugar

4 teaspoons baking powder

¼ teaspoon salt

1⅓ cups skim milk

1 large egg, lightly beaten

2 tablespoons vegetable oil, plus more for frying

½ pound fresh sweet cherries, pitted and sliced (1 cup)

Butter and maple syrup (optional)

◆ In a large bowl, combine the flour, cornmeal, sugar, baking powder, and salt. In a small bowl, combine the milk, egg, and 2 tablespoons of the oil. Immediately add the milk mixture to the flour mixture. Stir just until the dry ingredients are moistened. Gently fold in the cherries.

◆ Heat the oven to 200°F. Lightly oil a large skillet and place over medium heat. Spread about ½ cup batter on the griddle to make a 7-inch pancake. Cook until bubbles form and begin to break on the top surface. Turn the pancake over and cook until the bottom is golden brown. Remove the pancake and keep warm in the oven.

◆ Repeat with the remaining batter, adding more oil to the pan as necessary. Serve the pancakes warm, with the butter and syrup, if desired.

◆ BRING IT ALONG ◆

Prepared pancake batters can be transported to picnics if kept in the cooler. Bring the batter along in a food storage bag, and when time to cook, snip off the corner, squeeze out the batter onto a skillet. Once complete, serve the pancakes with syrup and fruit. Bring along a pancake turner and vegetable oil for cooking the pancakes.

Peachy Pancakes

Instead of peach yogurt, any flavor can be substituted in the batter of these pancakes. In place of or in addition to maple syrup, offer fruit syrups such as raspberry, blackberry, or blueberry.

MAKES 2 SERVINGS

1 cup unsifted all-purpose flour

1 tablespoon sugar

1 teaspoon baking powder

½ teaspoon baking soda

½ teaspoon salt

½ teaspoon ground nutmeg

1 large egg

1 8-ounce container lowfat peach yogurt

¼ cup water

1 tablespoon vegetable oil plus more for frying

½ teaspoon vanilla extract

Maple syrup (optional)

◆ In a large bowl, combine the flour, sugar, baking powder, baking soda, salt, and nutmeg, and set aside.

◆ In a medium-size bowl, with a wire whisk, beat together the egg, yogurt, water, 1 tablespoon of the oil, and the vanilla until the mixture is blended. Add the yogurt mixture to the flour mixture, gently stirring just until the dry ingredients are moistened.

◆ Heat the oven to 200°F. Lightly oil a griddle or 6-inch skillet and place over medium heat. Spread ¼ cup of batter onto the griddle to make a 4-inch pancake. Cook until bubbles form and begin to break on the top surface. Turn the pancake over and cook until the bottom is golden brown. Remove the pancake and keep warm on an ovenproof platter in the oven.

◆ Repeat with the remaining batter, adding more oil to the griddle as necessary. Serve the pancakes warm, with the maple syrup, if desired.

◆ A WEEKEND BRUNCH FOR A CROWD ◆

Raspberry Streusel Muffins, p. 14

Sweet-Cherry Pancakes, p. 25

Breakfast Tomatoes, p. 29

An Irish Fry, p. 32

Summer Fruit & Dip, p. 30

Iced Mint Tea, p. 178

Fruit-Stuffed French Toast with Orange Sauce

Any of your favorite fruits or berries can be used in this recipe. For large parties, multiply the recipe and cook the French toast in batches, keeping finished slices warm on an heatproof platter in a 250° F oven.

MAKES 4 SERVINGS

Orange Sauce

½ cup (1 stick) butter

⅓ cup sugar

2 oranges, peeled and thinly sliced

¼ cup freshly squeezed orange juice

¼ teaspoon cornstarch

French Toast

1 1-pound (about 8 inches long) rectangular loaf
    unsliced challah or egg bread

1 cup chopped or sliced fruit, such as red-fleshed
    papaya, mango, mamey, atemoya, or canistel

½ tablespoon vegetable oil

2 large eggs

1 cup milk

1 tablespoon orange-flavored liqueur

◆ Prepare the orange sauce: In a large skillet, melt the butter over medium-high heat. Add the sugar and cook until the mixture is bubbly. Add the orange slices and cook, stirring occasionally, for 5 minutes. In a 1-cup glass measuring cup or a small bowl, combine the orange juice and cornstarch. Add the juice mixture to the orange and sugar mixture in the skillet and cook, stirring constantly, until the sauce thickens slightly and becomes translucent. Remove the sauce from the heat, pour into a serving bowl, and keep warm.

◆ Prepare the French toast: With a bread knife, trim the short ends from the loaf. Cut the bread crosswise into four 1½-inch-thick slices. With a sharp knife, on one edge of each bread slice, make a horizontal incision to the center of the bread to create a pocket. Stuff each pocket with ¼ cup fruit, being careful not to poke a hole through the top or bottom of each bread slice.

◆ In a large skillet, heat the oil over medium heat. In a pie plate or wide-mouthed bowl, combine the eggs, milk, and liqueur. Dip each stuffed bread slice into the egg mixture until the bread is saturated. Reduce the heat to low and fry the bread slices, in batches if necessary, turning once, until browned on both sides—about 7 minutes on each side. Cut the slices in half diagonally and place 2 halves on each of 4 serving plates. Spoon the orange sauce over the french toast and serve warm.

Breakfast Tomatoes

Baked eggs with smoked-salmon hash are served in individual tomato containers, making them

perfect for parties. Double, triple, or quadruple this recipe and line the tomatoes on a warmed rimmed platter

for brunch. Serve them with a set of tongs and a large spoon.

MAKES 4 SERVINGS

4 large firm tomatoes

1 tablespoon butter or margarine

2 tablespoons finely chopped onion

2 teaspoons chopped fresh tarragon leaves or

½ teaspoon dried tarragon

1 teaspoon all-purpose flour

1 tablespoon milk

½ cup cubed unpeeled red potato, cooked until

just tender

1 ounce smoked salmon, coarsely chopped

(3 tablespoons chopped)

2 teaspoons chopped fresh parsley leaves

⅛ teaspoon ground black pepper

⅛ teaspoon salt

4 large eggs

Fresh tarragon sprigs (optional)

◆ With a sharp knife, trim off ¾ inch from the stem end of the tomatoes. Scoop the seeds and pulp out of the tomatoes into a strainer placed over a measuring cup. Set the tomato shells aside. Press the tomato pulp and seeds in the strainer to extract the tomato juice, and discard the remaining pulp and seeds.

◆ Heat the oven to 375°F. In a small skillet, melt the butter. Add the onion and chopped tarragon and sauté until the onion is golden. Stir in the flour and cook for 1 minute. With a wire whisk, beat the milk and ¼ cup of the strained tomato juice (use the remaining juice for another recipe) into the skillet. Heat the mixture to boiling, stirring constantly until it thickens. Remove the skillet from the heat.

◆ Stir the potato, salmon, parsley, pepper, and salt, if desired, into the mixture in the skillet. Divide the salmon hash evenly among the tomato shells. Place the tomatoes in a 9-inch round or square baking dish.

◆ Gently crack 1 egg into each filled-tomato shell, being careful not to break the yolk. Carefully cover the baking dish with a lid or aluminum foil. Bake the tomatoes for 20 to 25 minutes, or until the eggs are just cooked. Transfer to warmed serving plates, and top with the fresh tarragon sprigs, if desired. Serve immediately.

Summer Fruit & Dip

Homemade crème fraîche forms a dip for cherries, strawberries, and sugared currants. If you can find them, add some rosy-yellow Queen Anne cherries to the platter. On picnics, store the dip in the cooler until serving.

MAKES 8 SERVINGS

2 cups (1 pint) heavy cream (not ultra-pasteurized)

3 tablespoons buttermilk

4 cups (2 pints) strawberries

2 cups fresh sweet cherries

1 quart red currants or 1 pound small seedless
    red grapes, rinsed and dried, stems intact

1 envelope unflavored gelatin

½ cup water

2 tablespoons very cold water

1 teaspoon fruit-flavored liqueur

½ cup sugar

Currant or grape leaves (optional)

♦ One day before serving, combine the heavy cream and buttermilk in a 1-quart bowl. Cover loosely and let stand at room temperature for 12 to 24 hours, or until the mixture thickens and tastes slightly tangy. Cover and refrigerate until serving time. The mixture will keep, covered and refrigerated, for 1 to 2 weeks.

♦ Rinse the fruit and cut into small clusters, if necessary. In a small saucepan, soften the gelatin in the ½ cup water. Heat over low heat, stirring constantly, until the gelatin dissolves. Pour the gelatin mixture into a shallow bowl and stir in the 2 tablespoons cold water and the liqueur. Place the sugar in a plastic bag and dip clusters of the fruit first into the gelatin mixture and then into the sugar, shaking gently to coat. Set aside on waxed paper until the sugar coating dries—about 10 to 15 minutes. To serve, arrange the fruit on serving platters or in bowls and garnish with the leaves, if desired. Spoon the crème fraîche into a serving bowl and serve alongside the fruit.

Mixed-Fruit Granola

This healthful blend of oats, nuts, and dried fruits is a hearty breakfast. Set it out on the table with a pitcher of cold milk and an assortment of mixed fresh berries. Fill single-serving pouches with dry granola for an energizing snack.

MAKES 12 SERVINGS

2 cups quick rolled oats

¾ cup wheat germ

½ cup sliced natural almonds

½ cup honey

1 tablespoon vegetable oil

1 tablespoon water

1 teaspoon ground cinnamon

¼ teaspoon salt

⅔ cup chopped pitted dates

½ cup golden raisins

½ cup dried apricots

⅓ cup dried cranberries

¼ cup hulled sunflower seeds

◆ Heat the oven to 350°F. In a large bowl, combine the oats, wheat germ, almonds, honey, oil, water, cinnamon, and salt. Spread the mixture onto 2 baking sheets and bake for 15 minutes, stirring several times, until the mixture is a dark golden brown. Pack the mixture into a 9-inch-square baking pan and cool to room temperature.

◆ Break the oat mixture into pea-size chunks over a large bowl. Stir in the dates, raisins, apricots, cranberries, and sunflower seeds. Store in an airtight container.

Breakfast-in-Disguise Oatmeal Cookies

These wholesome cookies can accompany a brunch spread, be eaten on the run, or be packed up to munch on during morning hikes through the countryside. Dried fruits such as raisins, cherries, dates, or apricots can be mixed into the batter.

MAKES TWENTY-EIGHT 1½-INCH COOKIES

1 cup unsifted all-purpose flour

1 cup quick rolled oats

2 tablespoons finely chopped toasted walnuts

1 teaspoon ground cinnamon

½ teaspoon baking soda

¼ teaspoon baking powder

¼ teaspoon salt

¾ cup firmly packed light-brown sugar

2 large egg whites

2 tablespoons vegetable oil

2 tablespoons prune lekvar (prune puree) or
    apple butter

1 teaspoon vanilla extract

◆ Heat the oven to 375°F. Lightly grease a large baking sheet. In a medium-size bowl, combine the flour, oats, walnuts, cinnamon, baking soda, baking powder, and salt.

◆ In a large bowl, with an electric mixer on medium speed, beat the brown sugar, egg whites, oil, lekvar, and vanilla until well blended. Reduce the mixer speed to low and beat in the flour mixture just until it is combined.

◆ Drop tablespoonfuls of dough, about 1 inch apart, onto the greased baking sheet. Bake the cookies for 8 minutes, or until set but not browned. Cool the cookies on wire racks until slightly warm. While still warm, store in an airtight container to keep them moist.

An Irish Fry

Pile this hearty mélange of Irish treats—including potatoes, bangers (Irish breakfast sausages), breakfast pudding, bacon, and eggs—on a huge platter and serve with a big pot of strong coffee as a welcoming Sunday brunch to be enjoyed leisurely out on the porch. This makes especially fine fare on a cold winter morning before hitting the slopes.

MAKES 6 SERVINGS

4 medium-size baking potatoes

¼ cup (½ stick) butter

½ cup all-purpose flour

1 large egg

1 tablespoon chopped fresh parsley leaves

1 tablespoon chopped fresh chives

1¼ teaspoons salt

¾ teaspoon ground black pepper

Vegetable oil, for frying

12 pork bangers

6 slices Irish bacon

1 8-ounce package breakfast pudding, sliced
    into ¾-inch-thick rounds

3 medium-size tomatoes

6 large eggs

Fresh thyme sprigs (optional)

◆ Heat the oven to 200°F. In a 4-quart saucepan, cover the potatoes with water and heat to boiling. Cover the potatoes and cook for 25 minutes, or until fork-tender. Drain the potatoes and cool until easy to handle. Peel the potatoes and mash them in a large bowl with the butter. Stir in the flour, egg, parsley, chives, 1 teaspoon of the salt, and ½ teaspoon of the pepper, mixing until well blended. In a large skillet, heat 2 tablespoons of the oil over medium heat. Shape the potato mixture into twelve 2½-inch patties and fry, in batches, until golden brown on both sides, adding more oil as necessary. Place on a large ovenproof platter and keep warm in the oven.

◆ In a large skillet, heat just enough oil to thinly coat the bottom of the skillet over low heat. Add the bangers, arrange in a single layer, and cook, turning frequently, until browned on all sides. Remove the bangers to the platter with the potato pancakes. Add the bacon to the skillet and fry, turning frequently, until done. (Irish bacon does not become crispy when cooked; it has the texture and color of smoked ham.) Remove the bacon to the platter in the oven. Add the breakfast pudding to the skillet and cook, turning, until firm and browned on the cut sides. Remove to the hot platter.

◆ Cut the tomatoes crosswise in half and sprinkle with ⅛ teaspoon of the salt and ⅛ teaspoon of the pepper. Fry the tomatoes, cut side down, in the skillet until lightly browned (do not overcook—the tomatoes should retain their shape). Remove to the hot platter.

◆ Just before serving, fry the eggs, in batches, sunny-side up, or as desired. Transfer to the platter in the oven and top with the remaining ⅛ teaspoon each salt and pepper. Garnish the platter with fresh thyme, if desired, and serve immediately.

APPETIZERS

Outdoor parties—whether they be for two or for a crowd—deserve to start off with something special. The intention is to whet the appetite and establish the pace for a lingering repast. Whether you prepare a simple dip or an elaborate roulade, great beginnings set the stage for a memorable affair. Offer a single hors d'oeuvre as a prelude to your meal, or a medley of small bites for a cocktail party.

Hummus

Dips are always a party pleaser; they are easy to prepare, and can be served with a number of different "dippers." Set out colorful platters of crudites including sticks of carrot, celery, zucchini, yellow squash, bell pepper, and jicama, broccoli and cauliflower flowerettes, trimmed green beans, sugar snap or snow pea pods, halved cherry tomatoes. Toasted pita triangles, bagel chips, crackers, crostini, melba toast, sliced baguettes, homemade potato and tortilla chips, and flatbreads make great dippers as well.

MAKES ABOUT 1²/₃ CUPS

2 cups cooked or 1 16-ounce can chick-peas,
    drained

3 tablespoons tahini

2 tablespoons fresh lemon juice

1 clove garlic, finely chopped

½ teaspoon ground black pepper

¼ teaspoon salt (optional)

1 teaspoon chopped fresh parsley leaves (optional)

◆ In a food processor with the chopping blade, or in a large bowl using a potato masher, process or mash the chick-peas until a smooth paste forms.

◆ Add the tahini, lemon juice, garlic, pepper, and salt, if desired, and process or stir the mixture until all the ingredients are well combined.

◆ Transfer the spread to a serving bowl and sprinkle with the parsley, if desired. Serve immediately.

Ripe Olive Spread

A close relative to tapenade, this puree of black olives enlivened with garlic and fresh lime juice can be a dip or a base for canapes of small pumpernickel or rye bread rounds topped with diced tomatoes or sliced mushrooms.

MAKES ABOUT 1¼ CUPS

2 6- or 5¾-ounce cans pitted ripe olives,
    drained

1 tablespoon fresh lime juice

1 tablespoon olive oil

1 clove garlic, finely chopped

½ teaspoon ground black pepper

1 tablespoon chopped sweet red pepper (optional)

◆ In a food processor with the chopping blade, process the olives until they are very finely chopped.

◆ Add the lime juice, oil, garlic, and black pepper. Process the mixture until it is well combined.

◆ Transfer the spread to a serving bowl and serve or cover and refrigerate until ready to serve. Garnish the spread with the red pepper, if desired.

Smoky Eggplant Dip

Roasting eggplant renders a meltingly delicious, smoky treat that marries well with typical Mediterranean flavors of olive oil, parsley, lemon juice, and garlic. For flavorful, portable vegetarian sandwiches, fill pita pockets with a generous portion of dip, shredded lettuce, diced tomatoes and cucumbers.

MAKES ABOUT 1½ CUPS

1 1-pound eggplant

1 tablespoon sesame seeds

2 tablespoons chopped fresh parsley leaves

2 tablespoons olive oil

4 teaspoons fresh lemon juice

1 clove garlic, finely chopped

¼ teaspoon salt

◆ Heat the oven to 400°F and lightly grease a baking sheet. Cut the eggplant in half lengthwise and place it, cut side down, on the greased baking sheet. Bake the eggplant for 45 to 50 minutes, or until the flesh is tender and the skin is blackened. Set it aside until cool enough to handle.

◆ In a small dry skillet, toast the sesame seeds over medium heat for about 3 minutes.

◆ Peel the eggplant and discard the skin. (For a smokier flavor, include some of the charred skin in the dip.)

◆ In a food processor fitted with the chopping blade, or a large bowl using a potato masher, process or mash the eggplant, parsley, oil, lemon juice, garlic, and salt until just combined. Transfer the dip to a serving bowl and sprinkle with the sesame seeds. Serve immediately or cover and refrigerate to serve chilled.

Summer Salsa

Adjust the heat by adding more or less jalapeño to taste, or experiment with other fresh chiles such as poblano (hot), serrano (hotter), or habanero (hottest). Serve this salsa with tortilla chips, or as a topping for nachos or grilled fish fillets or chicken breasts.

MAKES 1½ CUPS

3 large tomatoes, chopped

2 green onions, chopped

1 clove garlic, finely chopped

1 fresh jalapeño, finely chopped

¼ cup chopped fresh cilantro leaves

1 tablespoon fresh lime juice

2 teaspoons olive oil

¼ teaspoon salt

◆ In a 1-quart resealable container, combine all the ingredients. Cover and shake gently to mix. Store, covered in the refrigerator, for up to 3 days.

Goat Cheese & Red-Pepper Roulade

This colorful roulade is a tasty vegetarian starter or entree. For picnics, keep the roulade whole, tightly wrapped in plastic wrap, and the sauce in a separate container. Refrigerate both for at least an hour before packing along with other cold items in the cooler. Slice the roulade just before serving and spoon a dollop of sauce over each slice.

MAKES 6 SERVINGS

5 large eggs

½ cup buttermilk

⅓ cup part-skim ricotta cheese

1 cup coarsely shredded lowfat Swiss cheese

1 tablespoon chopped fresh parsley leaves

1 tablespoon fresh thyme leaves or
    1 teaspoon dried thyme leaves

¼ teaspoon salt

⅛ teaspoon ground black pepper

1 tablespoon vegetable oil

1 small onion, chopped

2½ cups fresh spinach

½ cup milk

1 3-ounce package goat cheese

2 7-ounce jars roasted sweet-red peppers,
    drained

Fresh thyme sprigs (optional)

◆ Generously grease a 15½- by 10½-inch jelly-roll pan or shallow baking pan. Separate the eggs, placing the whites in a large bowl and the yolks in a small bowl.

◆ In a medium-size bowl, combine the buttermilk and ricotta until well mixed. Beat the egg yolks, one at a time, into the cheese mixture. Stir in the Swiss cheese, parsley, thyme, salt, and pepper.

◆ Place the rack in the center of the oven. Heat the oven to 350°F. With an electric mixer on high speed, beat the egg whites until stiff peaks form. Fold the cheese mixture into the egg whites just until blended. Pour the mixture into the greased pan, spreading it to the edges. Bake for 12 to 15 minutes, or just until firm in the center.

◆ Place a clean cotton or linen towel on a work surface and turn the baked roulade upside down onto the towel. Remove the jelly-roll pan. From a short edge, quickly roll up the roulade in the towel and cool to room temperature on a wire rack.

◆ Meanwhile, prepare the sauce: In a medium-size skillet, heat the oil over medium heat. Add the onion and sauté for 5 minutes. Reduce the heat to low and stir in the spinach until mixed. Cook the spinach mixture for 2 minutes, or until the spinach is wilted. Transfer the spinach mixture to a blender or food processor fitted with the chopping blade. Add the milk and process the mixture until a smooth puree forms. Set the sauce aside.

◆ Unroll the roulade and spread evenly with the goat cheese. Pat the red-pepper pieces dry on paper towels and arrange over the goat cheese to cover the entire surface. From a short edge, carefully roll up the roulade. Slice into 6 servings. Pour the sauce onto a serving platter. Arrange the roulade slices on the sauce and garnish with thyme sprigs, if desired.

Nachos with Black Beans

Served with with Turkey & Corn Fajitas, p. 93 pictured here, you will have a very full and simple Southwestern meal.

MAKES 4 SERVINGS

½ cup dried black beans (¼ pound)

1 tablespoon olive oil

1 large carrot, finely chopped

1 medium-size onion, finely chopped

1 stalk celery, finely chopped

3 cloves garlic, finely chopped

2½ cups water

2 teaspoons dried thyme leaves

1 teaspoon ground cumin

½ teaspoon salt

½ teaspoon grated lemon rind

½ teaspoon ground black pepper

1 17-ounce bag tortilla chips

1 large tomato, chopped

¼ pound Monterey Jack cheese, shredded

1 jalapeño pepper, seeded and sliced crosswise

◆ Several hours or the day before serving, sort and soak the beans following the package directions. Drain and rinse the beans.

◆ In a 2-quart saucepan, heat the oil over medium heat. Sauté the carrot, onion, celery, and garlic until the onion becomes transparent. Stir in the beans, water, thyme, cumin, salt, lemon rind, and black pepper. Heat the bean mixture to boiling over high heat. Reduce the heat to medium and cook until the beans are tender and the liquid has been absorbed—1½ to 2 hours.

◆ Heat the oven to 400°F. Place a layer of chips on an oven-safe serving plate. If using a microwave oven, place the chips on a microwave-safe serving plate. Evenly top the chips with the black beans, tomato, cheese, and jalapeño pepper. Bake for 5 minutes or heat in microwave on high (100 percent) for 1 minute, or until the cheese is melted. Serve immediately.

◆ STORING FOOD SAFELY ◆

When packing for picnics, always keep hot foods hot and cold foods cold to avoid bacterial contamination. Cold foods go in airtight plastic containers in an insulated cooler equipped with ice packs. You can retain heat by wrapping warm foods in heavy-duty aluminum foil, then in a towel, and nestling snugly in a basket. (Several companies make carriers with heat-reflective linings that keep foods warm.) Some housewares stores sell packs that can be microwaved and stowed alongside well-wrapped warm foods. Put foods out just before serving, and promptly store any leftovers. Thermoses are essential to retain the temperature of hot or cold drinks or soup. They are now widely available in a number of sizes, from pints to gallon-size jugs.

Tomato Tapenade in Squash Cups

Tomato tapenade, a cousin of traditional olive-and-caper tapenade, is redolent of Tuscany with ripe tomatoes, onion, garlic, and fresh oregano. Served in zucchini and summer squash cups, these tidbits are excellent finger food to pass at parties or a spring luncheon. A perfect beginning to a menu with Fresh Parsley Soup, p. 55 and Pepper-Crusted Filet Mignon Salad, p. 79, they can be assembled a day ahead on their serving platter or packed in layers with waxed paper between each layer in a flat-bottomed plastic container.

MAKES 24 FILLED SQUASH CUPS

Tomato Tapenade

1 tablespoon olive oil

½ cup finely chopped sweet red pepper

1 small onion, finely chopped

2 large (1 pound) tomatoes, skinned, seeded, and chopped

1 clove garlic, finely chopped

1 tablespoon fresh lemon juice

1 tablespoon white wine or water

2 teaspoons chopped fresh oregano leaves or ½ teaspoon dried oregano leaves

½ teaspoon sugar

¼ teaspoon salt

¼ teaspoon ground black pepper

5 ripe olives, pitted and finely chopped

Squash Cups

½ pound zucchini, not more than 1½ inches in diameter

½ pound yellow squash, not more than 1½ inches in diameter

24 toasted pine nuts

◆ The day before serving, prepare the tomato tapenade: In a large skillet, heat the oil. Add the red pepper and onion and cook until the onion is golden. Add the tomatoes, garlic, lemon juice, wine, oregano, sugar, salt, and pepper. Cook, covered, stirring often, until the vegetables are soft and most of the liquid has evaporated. Remove from the heat and stir in the olives. Cool completely. Cover with plastic wrap and refrigerate until ready to use.

◆ Several hours or the day before serving, prepare the squash cups: Cut the zucchini and yellow squash crosswise into twenty four ¾-inch-thick slices. With a small knife, cut out the pulp and seeds ½ inch deep from the center of each slice, creating a cup.

◆ In a 4-quart saucepan, heat 3 inches of water to boiling. Add the zucchini and yellow squash cups and cook for 1½ minutes. Drain the cups and rinse with cold water to cool. Pat the cups dry, wrap with plastic wrap, and refrigerate until ready to fill.

◆ Several hours or the day before serving, spoon 1 teaspoon of the tapenade into each squash cup and place on a tray or serving platter. Cover with plastic wrap and refrigerate until ready to serve. Just before serving, garnish each filled cup with 1 toasted pine nut.

Fruit-Stuffed Melon

Whole small melons become attractive natural serving bowls for a salad of macerated summer fruits topped with edible flowers. Use pesticide-free flowers for the garnish. For picnics, fill the melons with fruit salad, wrap each tightly with plastic wrap, and carry the flowers separately in an airtight plastic container. Transport everything in a cooler, making sure it snugly fits to avoid tipping the melons. Garnish each melon with flowers just before serving.

MAKES 4 SERVINGS

4 small ripe cantaloupes

Fresh seasonal fruits such as raspberries, strawberries,
  peaches, blackberries, figs, and pitted cherries

6 to 8 tablespoons sugar

¼ cup fruit-flavored liqueur, Muscat wine, or
  champagne

A handful of edible herb flowers such as nasturtiums,
  rosemary blossoms, marigold petals, sage blossoms,
  or rose petals

About 24 nasturtium flowers with stems

◆ Wipe the melons with a damp cloth. Use a sharp knife to cut across the top of each melon to make a round opening tablespoon-size. Remove and discard the seeds and scoop the flesh into a bowl, using either a melon-ball cutter or a teaspoon, taking care not to puncture the skin.

◆ Add a selection of the summer fruits, diced or sliced as appropriate, to the melon flesh and mix in the sugar. Pour the liqueur over the fruit and leave covered in a cold place for at least 30 minutes.

◆ Sprinkle the flower petals over the fruit and spoon it into the melon shells. Arrange some nasturtium flowers in the opening to conceal the fruit. In hot weather, serve the melons standing on beds of ice in shallow bowls.

GAMES FOR KIDS

To keep the children as well as grown-up kids amused, have an assortment of games on hand for picnics and porch suppers. Lawn games such as croquet, badminton, and horseshoes are classics that everyone can enjoy. You can set these games up in a matter of minutes with a minimal amount of equipment. Frisbees, kites, softballs and catchers mitts, footballs, and soccer balls are always fun and don't require formal teams. Remember hopscotch? Big sticks of colorful chalk can be used to create the course, and it is easily washed away with a quick spray from the garden hose. Old-fashioned favorites such as jacks and jump rope are perennial pleasers. Don't feel like packing games for picnics? Charades, 20 questions, hide and seek, relay races, duck-duck-goose, and monkey in the middle require little more than a willing crowd. Cards, puzzles, and books work indoors and out and are great for wind-down time.

Curried-Mushroom Crêpes

These scrumptious mushroom-filled crêpe bundles make elegant hors d'oeuvres for outdoor cocktail parties. Best of all, they are prepared ahead and refrigerated until serving, freeing up your time the day of the affair. For a dramatic touch, garnish the platter with pesticide-free edible flowers such as nasturtiums, pansies, or chive blossoms. Place the filled crêpes snugly in single layers in a flat, rectangular plastic container, with a sheet of waxed paper between each layer for traveling.

MAKES 24 CRÊPES

¾ cup unsifted all-purpose flour

¼ teaspoon salt

2 large eggs

1 cup milk

⅓ cup cooked wild rice

1 tablespoon vegetable oil

1 tablespoon butter or margarine

½ pound fresh shiitake mushrooms, cleaned, stemmed, and caps thinly sliced

2 tablespoons chopped shallots

2 tablespoons white wine

1 teaspoon curry powder

1 8-ounce package cream cheese, cut into cubes

⅓ cup heavy cream

2 teaspoons Dijon-style prepared mustard

24 fresh chives

Chopped fresh parsley leaves

◆ In a medium-size bowl, combine the flour and salt. With a wire whisk, beat in the eggs and milk until the mixture is almost smooth. Stir in the wild rice.

◆ Heat a heavy 9-inch skillet over medium heat. Brush the bottom with some of the oil. Spoon about ⅓ cup of the batter into the skillet and tip the pan to coat the bottom. Cook the crêpe for 2 minutes or until the top is set and the bottom is lightly browned. Carefully turn the crêpe and cook on the other side. Remove the finished crêpe to a sheet of waxed paper. Repeat to make 5 more crêpes, placing a sheet of waxed paper between each crepe. When all the crêpes are made, cover the stack tightly with plastic wrap and refrigerate for up to 2 days or seal in a plastic bag and freeze for up to 2 weeks.

◆ A day before serving, in a large skillet, melt the butter. Add the mushrooms and shallots and sauté until lightly browned. Stir in the wine and curry and cook until the wine evaporates. Add the cream cheese, cream, and mustard and cook until the cream cheese melts and the mixture thickens. Place in a small bowl, cover and refrigerate until the mixture is well chilled.

◆ With a 2¾-inch-round cutter, cut out 24 rounds from the crêpes. Place about 2 teaspoons of the filling onto the top half of each crêpe round. Fold the crêpe on each side over the filling so that the top of the round is open and the bottom is cone shaped. Tie a chive around the bottom half of the crêpe cone and trim the chive ends. Sprinkle the open ends of the cones with the chopped parsley and place on a tray or serving platter. Cover and refrigerate until ready to serve.

Citrus-Marinated Shrimp

By marinating cooked shrimp in a trio of fresh citrus juices they take on a delectably tart flavor. Pass around a platter for porch suppers, or for picnics transport the skewers in a single layer tightly fitted in a shallow plastic container; place the container at the bottom of your cooler to prevent it from tipping or sliding around.

MAKES 8 SERVINGS

3 large navel oranges

1 lemon

1 lime

1 tablespoon sugar

¼ teaspoon salt

2 tablespoons olive oil

3 cloves garlic, finely chopped

24 (about ¾ pound) large shrimp, shelled and deveined, leaving the last tail segment attached

SUMMERTIME SEAFOOD SUPPER

Citrus-Marinated Shrimp

Swordfish Brochettes, p. 106

Herbed Orzo Salad, p. 65

Grilled Vegetables

Bourbon Carrot Cake, p. 170

Carambola Cooler, p. 183

◆ Eight hours or 1 day ahead, marinate the shrimp: To make the marinade, with a zester, remove strips of peel from 1 orange, the lemon, and lime. Place the strips in a small saucepan with enough water to cover. Heat to boiling, cook for 1 minute, and drain. Place the strips in a large resealable bag or container. Cut the zested orange, lemon, and lime crosswise in half, ream or squeeze to extract all the juices, and add to the peel in the saucepan. Add the sugar and salt to the juice mixture and set aside.

◆ In a large skillet, heat the oil over medium heat. Add the garlic and sauté for 30 seconds. Add the shrimp and cook just until pink and cooked through—4 to 5 minutes. Set aside to cool slightly. Add the shrimp, the pan juices and garlic to the marinade mixture. Seal the bag and gently shake to coat the shrimp with the marinade. Refrigerate the shrimp mixture for 8 hours or overnight.

◆ To serve, peel the remaining 2 oranges and cut each orange into twenty four ½-inch chunks. Using toothpicks, spear each shrimp, tail end up. Stand each shrimp on an orange chunk and arrange on a serving platter. Garnish with some of the citrus-peel strips.

Mussels Provençal

Better to serve this dish at home, where the mussels will go straight from your broiler to the table. They should be eaten immediately to savor all the juices.

MAKES 4 SERVINGS

2 pounds fresh mussels

1 cup dry white wine

½ cup finely grated fresh bread crumbs

¼ cup finely chopped fresh parsley leaves

3 large cloves garlic, finely chopped

⅛ teaspoon salt

⅛ teaspoon ground black pepper

2 tablespoons olive oil

◆ With a stiff brush, scrub the mussel shells and tear the beard off each mussel. Rinse the mussels thoroughly under cold running water. In a 10-inch skillet, combine the mussels and wine. Cover the skillet and heat the wine to boiling over high heat. Reduce the heat to medium and steam the mussels until the shells open—5 to 8 minutes. With tongs, remove the mussels to rimmed baking sheets, discarding any unopened mussels. Reserve the cooking liquid in the skillet.

◆ Heat the broiler. Snap off and discard 1 shell from each mussel. In a small bowl, combine the bread crumbs, parsley, garlic, salt, and pepper. Stir in the oil until the mixture is evenly combined. Spoon the crumb mixture over the mussels, dividing evenly, and drizzle with 3 tablespoons reserved cooking liquid.

◆ Broil the mussels 4 inches from the heat, watching constantly, 4 to 5 minutes, or until golden brown. Transfer to a serving dish and serve immediately.

Corn & Crab Cakes with Summer Salad

Here's a perfect summertime first course that requires very little cooking. Use the sweetest corn you can find and only bright, ripe tomatoes for the salad.

MAKES 6 SERVINGS

Summer Salad

3 ears fresh yellow corn, shucked and silk removed

3 large tomatoes, diced

1 small red onion, finely chopped

1 tablespoon olive oil

2 teaspoons balsamic vinegar

¼ teaspoon salt

Corn & Crab Cakes

1 pound fresh or pasteurized lump crabmeat

1 cup fresh bread crumbs

2 large eggs

¼ cup mayonnaise

¼ cup finely chopped sweet red pepper

3 tablespoons chopped fresh parsley leaves

2 tablespoons fresh lemon juice

2 tablespoons prepared mustard

1 tablespoon chopped fresh dill

½ teaspoon crab-boil seasoning

Dash hot red-pepper sauce

1 tablespoon olive oil

1 tablespoon butter

12 ears fresh baby corn, shucked and silk removed
   (optional)

4 cups mixed chilled salad greens

♦ Make the summer salad: With a sharp knife, cut the corn from the cobs. Reserve ½ cup corn for the crab cakes. In a medium-size bowl, combine the remaining corn, the tomatoes, onion, 1 tablespoon oil, vinegar, and salt. Cover and refrigerate while preparing the crab cakes.

♦ Prepare the corn & crab cakes: On a plate or in a pie plate, pick through the crabmeat to remove any bits of shell and cartilage. In a medium-size bowl, stir together the bread crumbs, eggs, mayonnaise, red pepper, parsley, lemon juice, mustard, dill, crab-boil seasoning, red-pepper sauce, and reserved ½ cup corn until well combined. Gently fold in the crabmeat. Divide mixture into 6 portions, form each into a 3-inch cake.

♦ In a large skillet, heat the 1 tablespoon oil and the butter over medium heat. In batches, sauté the crab cakes until golden brown on both sides—about 5 minutes.

♦ To cook the baby corn, if desired, in a 2-quart saucepan, heat about 4 inches of water to boiling. Add the baby corn and cook for 3 minutes. Drain and cool to room temperature.

♦ To serve, arrange the salad greens on 6 dinner plates; spoon the summer salad over the greens. Place 1 crab cake on each salad and garnish with the baby corn, if desired. Serve immediately.

IMPROMPTU
PICNICS

Occasionally, the best times occur on the spur of the moment. Even the barest pantry always has something to rustle together. Throw a loaf of bread, a wedge of cheese, a bar of chocolate, and a bottle of wine in a picnic basket and you've got the makings of a romantic interlude reminiscent of dining alfresco along the Left Bank in Paris.

◆ Jars of pickles, roasted sweet red peppers, olives, marinated artichoke hearts or mushrooms, and cubes of mozzarella, asiago, or sharp provolone suddenly become antipasto. Layer them in a plastic container with a tight-fitting lid.

◆ Crisp crackers or crostini, a round of goat cheese, and a jar or sundried tomatoes are the makings of a scrumptious snack. Wrap each separately and toss into a back-pack with some napkins and bottled water.

◆ Try filling a baguette with slices of mozzarella or brie, fresh basil and sliced tomatoes from the garden. Top

with a drizzle of honey mustard, wrap in aluminum foil, and bring along a large knife and a cutting board. Once at your destination, unwrap the sandwich, slice and serve on the cutting board.

◆ Pair leftover cooked chicken with arugula and tomatoes in pita pockets, or stuff a pita with salad, dressing and a slice of cheese. Wrap each pita individually in aluminum foil, and to prevent them from getting crushed, put them upright in a plastic container with a tight-fitting lid.

◆ Layer deli-sliced turkey, roast beef, or steak with horseradish, thin slices of red onion and ripe tomato rolled up in lavash for an easily portable feast.

SOUPS
&
SALADS

Soups and salads are the very best way to enjoy the season's harvest. Recipes are easily adapted depending on what's available, for an infinite variety. There's nothing like a steaming hot bowl of hearty soup to warm you up on a cool evening, or a light, fragrant icy chilled soup to cool you on a hot summer day.

Soups and salads go hand-in-hand with outdoor entertaining since they can be prepared ahead and are easy to transport. Be sure to balance your soups and salads, a light salad needs a heavy soup to fill you up.

Corn Rivvel Soup

Rivvels are homemade dumpling-like noodles that turn this corn soup into an old-fashioned delight. Because of the rivvels, this soup is better served immediately after cooking.

MAKES 6 SERVINGS

Chicken Soup

2 pounds chicken necks and backs

5 cups water

1 medium-size onion, coarsely chopped

1 teaspoon salt

⅛ teaspoon ground black pepper

Egg Rivvels

1 cup unsifted all-purpose flour

¼ teaspoon salt

1 large egg, lightly beaten

2 cups (4 ears) fresh or frozen white- or yellow
  whole-kernel corn

1 tablespoon chopped fresh parsley leaves

◆ Prepare the chicken soup: In a 5-quart kettle, combine the chicken, water, onion, salt, and pepper. Heat to boiling over high heat. Reduce the heat to low and cover. Cook the chicken broth for 30 minutes. With a slotted spoon, remove the chicken pieces to a plate. Set aside the chicken until cool enough to handle. Skim the fat from the soup in the kettle.

◆ Prepare the egg rivvels: In a medium-size bowl, combine the flour, salt, and egg. Stir with a fork until the mixture forms a crumbly dough. Pick up small pieces of the dough and roll between your fingers or on the palm of your hand to make small, oval lumps. Repeat until all the rivvels are formed.

◆ Remove the chicken meat from the bones, discard the bones, and return the meat to the soup. Add the corn and heat to boiling over high heat. Reduce the heat to low and simmer the soup for 5 minutes. Add the rivvels and simmer for 10 minutes longer. Sprinkle with the parsley and serve immediately.

Fresh Parsley Soup

As this bright green soup cooks quickly, it is a snap to prepare for spur-of-the-moment porch suppers or picnics.

MAKES 2 SERVINGS

¼ cup finely chopped onion

1 tablespoon butter

2 cups half-and-half

2 tablespoons all-purpose flour

½ teaspoon salt

¾ cup chopped fresh parsley

◆ In a heavy 1-quart saucepan, sauté the onion in the butter until tender. In a cup, stir together ½ cup of the half-and-half, the flour, and salt until smooth. Add to the onion along with the remaining 1½ cups half-and-half. Cook, stirring, until boiling and thickened. Stir in the parsley and serve.

Tomato Soup with Fennel

Served chilled, tomato soup is a cool start to dinner on a hot night and is ideal for picnics. Pack the melba toast separately and the soup in a thermos jug or plastic container with a tight-fitting lid.

MAKES 4 SERVINGS

12 thin slices white bread

1 medium-size bulb fennel, tops reserved, chopped

4 medium-size tomatoes, peeled, seeded, and chopped

¾ cup buttermilk

½ teaspoon salt

¼ teaspoon ground white pepper

◆ Heat the oven to 325°F. Flatten the bread to ⅛-inch thickness. Cut the bread into 3½-inch squares. Arrange on baking sheets and bake for 8 minutes. Turn the slices and bake for 7 minutes longer, or until the bread is brown.

◆ In a 2-quart saucepan, combine the fennel and tomatoes. Heat to boiling over medium-high heat. Cover and reduce the heat to low. Simmer, stirring occasionally, until very tender—about 45 minutes.

◆ In a food processor fitted with the chopping blade, or in a blender, puree the fennel mixture until smooth. Strain the mixture into a medium-size bowl, reserving the liquid and discarding any solids left in the strainer.

◆ Chop some of the reserved fennel top, reserving some whole sprigs for garnish. Stir the chopped fennel top, the buttermilk, salt, and pepper into the fennel mixture. Refrigerate at least 24 hours.

◆ Spoon the chilled soup into a serving bowl and garnish with the reserved fennel sprigs. Serve with the toast.

BRINGING OUT YOUR BEST

To get the best ideas for picnics, attend an outdoor concert and check out your neighbors dining on the lawn. The "regulars" in attendance often seem to vie for the best picnic setup. Witnessed one evening at an outdoor venue: a low table placed on an Oriental rug and set with a crisp lace tablecloth with matching napkins, crystal wine goblets, silver place settings, fine bone china, sterling candlesticks with beeswax candles, and a crystal vase overflowing with wildflowers. Pity the poor soul who had to carry all of this! However, one need not go to such extremes to create an elegant affair—a pretty table linen, cloth napkins, glasses, plates, candles, and fresh flowers (bunched in a tall cup) makes a special presentation.

Several companies make sturdy reusable plastic cups, plates, and utensils that are attractive as well as light enough to pack and (perhaps more importantly) unbreakable. Bring light folding chairs and pillows for people to languish on. Bring along some comfortable pillows, a small blanket or throw if dining at night, un umbrella to shade your guests, and a wine bucket for any kind of bottled beverage.

Red-Pepper Potato Soup

Here's a clever way to put a heart-shaped cookie cutter to use for a romantic candlelit porch dinner. Placing the cutter in the center of a bowl creates a well for the red-pepper soup, around which you pour white-potato soup to create a heartfelt presentation. The trick is to assemble this soup at the table so you don't upset the design when transporting it. On picnics, carry the garnish in a small container and the two soups in separate thermoses. Pour some potato soup in each bowl, top with some red-pepper soup in the center, and use a knife to create a swirl design (or bring along the cookie cutter!).

MAKES 2 SERVINGS

¼ pound baking potatoes, peeled and cut into
   ½-inch cubes

¼ cup coarsely chopped onion

1 cup chicken broth

2 cups half-and-half

3 tablespoons all-purpose flour

¼ teaspoon salt

1 small sweet red pepper, seeded and quartered

Red food coloring (optional)

1 teaspoon chopped fresh dill or ¼ teaspoon
   dried dillweed

◆ In a heavy medium-size saucepan, cook the potatoes and onion in the chicken broth until soft—about 15 minutes. In the container of a blender, or in a food processor fitted with the chopping blade, puree the potatoes, onion, and broth. Return the mixture to the saucepan and set aside.

◆ In a small bowl, beat 1½ cups of the half-and-half into the flour until smooth. Add to the potato mixture in the saucepan. Stir in the salt. Heat to boiling over high heat, stirring constantly, until thickened. Reduce the heat and simmer for 3 minutes.

◆ Without washing the blender or food processor, place ⅔ cup of the potato soup and the red pepper in the container and process until smooth. Add the food coloring, if desired. In a small saucepan, reheat the soup, if necessary. Add the remaining half-and-half to the potato soup. Reheat, if necessary.

◆ Place a 1-inch-deep, 3-inch-wide, heart-shaped cookie cutter with an open top into the center of a shallow soup plate. Press tightly to the bottom of the plate. Pour half of the red-pepper soup inside the cookie cutter. Pour half of the potato soup around the outside of the cookie cutter. Very carefully remove the cutter by pulling straight up. Sprinkle the soup with the dill. Repeat to make a second serving. Serve immediately.

Mushroom-Potato Soup

This hearty, intensely flavored soup is a warm, welcoming start to supper on a frosty night. The wild mushrooms in the garnish are increasingly available in the produce section of major supermarkets, or in Asian markets. For picnics, pack the soup in a thermos and the mushroom and chive garnishes separately in plastic containers.

MAKES 6 SERVINGS

¼ cup (½ stick) butter or margarine

¼ pound fresh wild mushrooms (porcini,
    shiitake, chanterelle, or oyster), cleaned and
    stemmed, thinly sliced

¾ pound fresh white mushrooms, cleaned and sliced

1 small onion, sliced

2 teaspoons fresh lemon juice

2 medium-size (¾ pound) potatoes, peeled and sliced

2 10¾-ounce cans condensed chicken broth, undiluted

⅓ cup unsifted all-purpose flour

¼ teaspoon salt

¼ teaspoon ground black pepper

3 cups half-and-half

1 tablespoon chopped fresh chives or parsley leaves

◆ In a heavy 4-quart saucepan, melt half of the butter. Add the wild mushrooms and sauté just until tender. Remove the mushrooms with a slotted spoon or spatula to a bowl and set aside. Add the remaining 2 tablespoons butter, the white mushrooms, the onion, and lemon juice to the saucepan. Cook until the onions are golden brown. Add the potatoes and 1 can of the broth. Cook until the potatoes are tender—about 10 minutes.

◆ In a small bowl, very gradually stir the remaining 1 can broth into the flour until smooth. Stir the flour mixture, salt, and pepper into the potato mixture in the saucepan. Heat to boiling over high heat, stirring constantly, until the mixture thickens. Reduce the heat to low and cook for 5 minutes.

◆ In a blender, or in a food processor fitted with the chopping blade, puree the soup, one half at a time, until smooth. Return the soup to the saucepan. Stir in the half-and-half and heat just until boiling. Remove from the heat and ladle the soup into a tureen or individual bowls. Top with the reserved wild mushrooms and chopped chives. Serve immediately.

**WARM-YOUR-HEART
PORCH SUPPER
FOR A WINTRY NIGHT**

Mushroom-Potato Soup

Lamb Ragout with Couscous, p. 103

Steamed Spinach

Colonial Apple Pie, p. 172

Hot Spiced Tea, p. 178

Turkey Chowder in Phyllo

Here's a novel way to use leftover turkey and end up with a hearty meal. A crisp phyllo crust draped over turkey chowder helps the soup stay warm while dining outdoors and keeps spills to a minimum while transporting it. Fresh phyllo dough is available in the refrigerator section of many supermarkets.

MAKES 6 SERVINGS

1 tablespoon olive oil

1 10-ounce package cremini or other
    fresh cultivated exotic mushrooms, sliced

1 medium-size onion, chopped

6 cups turkey broth

4 cups ¾-inch pieces cooked turkey

1 pound small red potatoes, quartered

4 teaspoons chopped fresh dill or
    1 teaspoon dried dillweed

½ teaspoon salt (optional)

¼ teaspoon ground black pepper

1 cup half-and-half

2 tablespoons all-purpose flour

3 tablespoons unseasoned bread crumbs

¾ pound (18 leaves) fresh phyllo

6 tablespoons (¾ cup) butter, melted

1 large egg, lightly beaten

◆ In a 5-quart saucepot, heat the oil over medium heat. Add the mushrooms and onion and sauté until they are golden brown. Add the broth, turkey, potatoes, 1 teaspoon fresh dill or ¼ teaspoon dillweed, salt, if desired, and the pepper. Cover the saucepot and cook for 15 minutes, or until the potatoes are just tender. Remove the saucepot from the heat and set aside.

◆ Meanwhile, in a 1-cup glass measuring cup, combine the half-and-half and flour and stir until it is smooth. Stir into the broth mixture and cook, stirring, until the chowder thickens. Cook for 5 minutes longer. Remove from the heat.

◆ Heat the oven to 400°F. In a small bowl, combine the bread crumbs and 2 teaspoons fresh dill or ½ teaspoon dillweed. Place the phyllo between 2 sheets of waxed paper, then cover with a damp towel. (Phyllo dries out very quickly, so be sure to cover the remaining sheets each time you remove one.) Remove 1 sheet of the phyllo and lay it on a clean, flat surface. Brush the phyllo completely with butter and sprinkle with some of the bread crumb mixture. Repeat with 4 more sheets of phyllo. Top with 1 more sheet of phyllo and brush with the butter.

◆ Using 1 of six 1½- to 2-cup ovenproof soup bowls as a cutting guide, invert the bowl onto the stacked phyllo. With a sharp knife, cut a round from the stacked phyllo ¾ inch larger all around than the rim of the bowl. Set the bowl aside. Cut an X in the center of the round. Repeat to cut another round. Set the scraps aside. Cover the phyllo with the waxed paper and a damp towel and set aside. Repeat the process to make 2 more stacks, cutting out 4 more rounds.

◆ Divide the chowder among the 6 bowls. Sprinkle with the remaining 1 teaspoon of fresh dill or ¼ teaspoon of dillweed. Brush the rims of the bowls with the egg. Place a stacked phyllo round on top of each bowl. With scissors,

make 10 evenly spaced ½-inch-deep cuts around the edge of each phyllo round. Brush the cut phyllo edge with the egg, using the brush to press the phyllo down onto the bowl to seal.

◆ With scissors, cut the phyllo scraps into strips 1 inch longer than the diameter of the bowl, and twist or cut the

phyllo scraps into 2-inch square. Pinch in the center. Use the egg to seal twisted strips or pinched squares on the phyllo. Place the bowls on 2 rimmed baking sheets.

◆ Bake the chowder for 5 to 8 minutes or until the phyllo crust is golden brown. Remove from the oven and serve the chowder immediately.

Soupe de Poisson

One taste of this soup—redolent of seafood, garlic, tomatoes, saffron, wine, and thyme—and guests will be immediately transported from your porch to the Provencal countryside. Slices of toasted baguette spread with garlicky rouille and sprinkled with Gruyère float atop the soup, making this a meal in one bowl. If you prefer a chunkier version, don't puree the soup.

MAKES 6 SERVINGS

3 tablespoons extra-virgin olive oil

2 large (about 2 pounds) Spanish onions, halved and sliced

2½ pounds ripe tomatoes

6 cloves garlic, finely chopped

2 bay leaves

1 teaspoon fennel seeds

1 teaspoon dried thyme leaves

½ teaspoon salt

¾ teaspoon saffron threads, crushed

¼ teaspoon ground black pepper

2 pounds small red snapper, sea bass, or trout

4 cups water

1 cup dry white wine

¼ teaspoon ground red pepper

½ cup mayonnaise

18 ½-inch-thick slices French bread

½ pound skinless monkfish, flounder, or halibut fillets

6 ounces Gruyère cheese, finely shredded (¾ cup)

Fresh thyme sprigs (optional)

◆ In an 8-quart saucepot, heat the oil over medium-high heat. Add the onions and sauté them until they are well browned—about 10 minutes.

◆ Cut the tomatoes in half and squeeze out and discard the seeds. Cut the tomato halves into 1-inch chunks. Add the tomatoes, 4 cloves of the garlic, bay leaves, fennel seeds, thyme, salt, ½ teaspoon of the saffron, and the pepper to the onions and sauté until the tomatoes have softened and released their juices—about 5 minutes.

◆ Cut the heads off of the fish and set aside. Cut the fish crosswise into 1½-inch-wide slices. Add the fish heads and slices, the water, and wine to the tomato mixture. Heat to boiling over high heat, stirring frequently. Reduce the heat to medium, partially cover, and cook for 30 minutes.

◆ In a small bowl, with the back of a spoon, mash the remaining 2 cloves garlic, the remaining ¼ teaspoon of the saffron, and the red pepper together. Stir in the mayonnaise until blended. Cover tightly and refrigerate until ready to serve.

◆ Toast the bread slices on both sides and set aside.

◆ Strain the soup, 1 cup at a time, through a large sieve into a 4-quart saucepan. Remove the fish slices and set aside. Pressing with the back of a spoon, extract as much liquid from the solids as possible. Discard the solids.

Cut the fish fillets into 1-inch chunks and add to the hot soup. Heat just to boiling over medium-high heat. Remove the soup from the heat. In a blender, puree the soup, in batches, until smooth. Reheat the soup gently over low heat, just until hot.

To serve, ladle the soup into individual soup bowls. Spread the toast with some of the mayonnaise mixture. Place 3 slices on top of each soup bowl and sprinkle with the grated cheese. Garnish with the thyme sprigs, if desired. Serve the soup immediately.

Herbed Orzo Salad

This rice-like pasta salad is bathed in aromatic fresh basil, garlic, and pine nuts—flavors reminiscent of classic pesto without all the fuss. For more variety, add any of the following: cherry tomatoes, fresh sugar snap pea pods, diced red onion, steamed asparagus tips, blanched broccoli or cauliflower flowerettes, julienned zucchini or yellow squash, or sliced green onion. This dish is perfect for picnics since it can accompany almost anything; and since it contains no mayonnaise there is very little chance of spoilage. However, be safe and keep it in the cooler until just prior to serving.

MAKES 12 SERVINGS

1 16-ounce package orzo

3 tablespoons olive oil

3 cloves garlic, sliced

2 tablespoons packed thinly sliced fresh basil leaves

¼ cup lightly toasted pine nuts

2 tablespoons packed thinly sliced fresh
    flat-leaf parsley leaves

¼ teaspoon salt

⅛ teaspoon ground black pepper

◆ Several hours before serving, in a 4-quart saucepan, cook the orzo following the package directions.

◆ Meanwhile, in a small skillet, heat the oil and garlic over medium heat. Cook for 3 to 4 minutes or until the garlic slices are browned. Remove and discard the garlic slices, and set the garlic-flavored oil aside.

◆ Return the orzo to the same saucepan. Set aside about 1 teaspoon of the sliced basil leaves. Add the remaining basil, the garlic-flavored oil, the pine nuts, parsley, salt, and pepper. Toss the salad gently to combine.

◆ Transfer the salad to a large serving bowl and cool to room temperature. Sprinkle with the remaining 1 teaspoon basil and cover and refrigerate until cold—at least 1 hour. To pack for a picnic, tightly cover the bowl and transport in an insulated carrier.

Mushroom & Barley Salad

The woodsy flavors of mushrooms pair with crisp greens, nutty barley, and a thyme-and-lemon dressing in this satisfying salad. For picnics, pack the greens and tomatoes separately and assemble just before serving.

MAKES 6 SERVINGS

Mushroom & Barley Salad

2½ cups water

¾ cup pearl barley

1 tablespoon plus 1 teaspoon fresh thyme leaves

¼ teaspoon salt

2 tablespoons olive oil

1 clove garlic, finely chopped

2 ounces shiitake mushrooms, stemmed and sliced

½ teaspoon finely grated lemon rind

⅛ teaspoon ground black pepper

6 ounces assorted cultivated wild mushrooms
(such as oyster, chanterelle, or hedgehog), stemmed

½ cup yellow whole-kernel corn

Lemon-Thyme Dressing

⅓ cup olive oil

¼ cup white-wine vinegar

1 small clove garlic

2 tablespoons fresh lemon juice

1 teaspoon fresh thyme leaves

⅛ teaspoon salt

6 cups mixed salad greens, such as mâche, baby red-leaf
lettuce, Boston lettuce, or arugula

12 cherry tomatoes, halved

Fresh thyme sprig (optional)

◆ Prepare the mushroom & barley salad: In a 2-quart saucepan, heat the water to boiling. Add the barley, 1 teaspoon thyme, and the salt. Cook, tightly covered, over medium-low heat for 45 minutes or until the barley is tender and the liquid is absorbed. Spoon the barley into a medium-size bowl, cover, and set aside to cool to room temperature.

◆ In a large skillet, heat the oil over medium-high heat. Add the garlic and sauté until golden brown. Add the shiitake mushrooms, remaining 1 tablespoon thyme, the lemon rind, and pepper and cook, stirring occasionally, until the mushrooms soften—about 5 minutes. Add the assorted mushrooms and cook, stirring gently, until they are just tender—about 2 minutes. Set aside about ½ cup of the cooked mushrooms in a small bowl. Add the corn to the skillet and cook, stirring, until the corn is cooked— about 1 to 2 minutes. Transfer the mixture to the bowl with the barley.

◆ Prepare the lemon-thyme dressing: In a food processor fitted with the chopping blade, process the oil, vinegar, garlic, lemon juice, thyme, and salt until the mixture thickens.

◆ To serve, place the greens in a large serving bowl or on a platter. Spoon the barley mixture on top. Scatter the reserved ½ cup mushrooms on the mixture and place the cherry tomatoes around the edge of the bowl on the greens. Drizzle the lemon-thyme dressing over the salad and garnish with the fresh thyme, if desired.

A PICNIC
ON THE BEACH

Ahhh, a day at the beach. No one ever wants it to end, so why not extend the afternoon into evening, enjoying the late sun glistening as it sets over the water. The fresh salt air, gentle breezes carrying the slightest hint of ocean spray, all accompanied by the rhythmic crashing of the waves, provide the perfect atmosphere for a languid meal.

Simple foods already prepared work best at the beach to avoid a sandy repast. Try an early morning walk on the beach, bring along handkerchief-pouches of Mixed-Fruit Granola, p. 30. Or, for lunch, have a sampler of salads along with individually wrapped sandwiches, a bottle of wine, a jug of punch, bags of chips, some fruit, and a batch of cookies. Don't forget cups, plates, lots of napkins, a corkscrew, and garbage bags.

If dining at night, pack some Tomato Soup with Fennel, p. 55 in thermoses, Pepper-Crusted Filet Mignon Salad, p. 79, and Marinated Vegetable Kabobs, p. 118. Served with some crusty bread, you are sure to have a memorable meal watching the sun set. Be sure to bring along candles with hurricane shades, and find out if you can have a bonfire. If so, bring along matches, newspapers to start the fire, and marshmallows to toast.

Bacon, Lettuce, & Tomato Salad

The classic BLT is reborn as a salad. Instead of mayo "on the side" in little paper cups, everyone gets their own dressing in a little red-onion cup! The salad should be assembled beforehand—place the dressing in a small lidded container, wrap the onion cups separately in aluminum foil (so they retain their shape) and fill just before serving. Carry the cooled toasted bread in a resealable plastic bag.

MAKES 4 SERVINGS

Sour Cream-Chive Dressing

⅓ cup reduced-fat mayonnaise dressing

⅓ cup sour cream

¼ cup water

1 tablespoon cider vinegar

⅛ teaspoon salt

2 medium-size red onions

1 tablespoon finely chopped fresh chives (optional)

Bacon Salad

1 1-pound package thick-sliced bacon

6 cups torn mixed greens, such as endive, watercress, and green-leaf lettuce

1½ pounds cherry tomatoes, preferably with stems

1 large hard-cooked egg, finely chopped

1 small yellow tomato, chopped (optional)

8 slices toasted French bread

◆ Prepare the sour cream-chive dressing: In a small bowl, whisk together the mayonnaise, sour cream, water, vinegar, and salt, and set aside. Cut the red onions crosswise in half. To make the onion cups, cut and scoop out each onion half, leaving the bottom intact and about a ¼-inch-thick shell. Finely chop enough of the scooped-out onions to make ¼ cup. (Wrap and refrigerate any leftover onion for another use.) Add the chopped onion to the mayonnaise mixture. Fill the red-onion cups with the dressing, garnish with the chives, if desired, and refrigerate while preparing the salad.

◆ Prepare the bacon salad: Heat a large skillet over medium-high heat. Roll up each slice of bacon, starting at a short end. Stand each bacon roll on an end in the hot skillet. Cook for 3 to 4 minutes to brown; drain the fat from the skillet, holding the rolls in place with a saucepan lid.

◆ With metal tongs, carefully turn each bacon roll over and cook for 5 minutes, or until browned. Transfer the bacon rolls to a paper towel to drain.

◆ To arrange the salad, place 1½ cups of the greens on each serving plate and cluster some of the cherry tomatoes beside the greens. Top the greens with the bacon, the chopped egg, and the chopped yellow tomato, if desired. Place the filled red-onion cups and 2 slices of toasted bread on each plate. Serve.

Spinach Salad with Bacon Dressing

Corn roasted in the husk adds a smoky sweet flavor to this spinach salad. For picnics, pack the corn and spinach in a large food storage bag, the pine nuts separately in a small one, and the dressing in a jar with a tight-fitting lid. Just before serving, sprinkle the spinach mixture with the pine nuts, and shake the jar of dressing vigorously before pouring over the salad.

MAKES 10 SERVINGS

3 cups unsifted all-purpose flour

1 cup corn flour (masa harina)

2 tablespoons baking powder

2 tablespoons chopped fresh dill

1 teaspoon salt

2½ cups water

2 tablespoons olive oil

¾ cup yellow cornmeal

4 ears fresh yellow corn in husks

1 pound slab bacon, finely chopped

1 cup finely chopped red onions

⅓ cup rice-wine vinegar

2 tablespoons honey

2 tablespoons Dijon-style prepared mustard

⅓ cup blackberry brandy or apple juice

1 pound fresh spinach leaves, stems removed

1 cup toasted pine nuts

Rinsed and dried pesticide-free calendula flowers and
    chive blossoms (optional)

◆ In a large bowl, combine the flour, corn flour, baking powder, dill, and salt. Stir in the water until a thick batter forms. Cover and refrigerate for 1 hour. In an 8-inch skillet, heat the oil over medium-high heat. Spread the cornmeal into a thick layer on a clean work surface. Scoop out a heaping ¼ cup of the batter and place on the cornmeal. Sprinkle cornmeal on top of the batter and pat into a 5-inch round. Carefully transfer the round to a skillet and fry until lightly browned and puffy on each side—about 2 minutes per side. Drain the bread on paper towels. Repeat with remaining batter to make 9 more rounds.

◆ Heat the oven to 400°F. Carefully pull back the husks from the ears of corn, keeping them attached at the stem end. Remove the silk from the ears, then replace the husks. (If necessary, tie a wet cotton string around each ear to keep the husks in place.) Roast the corn in the husks for 25 minutes and set aside to cool.

◆ Meanwhile, in a large skillet, fry the bacon over medium heat until lightly browned, though not yet crisp. Drain off all but about 1 tablespoon of the bacon fat. Return the skillet to the heat and add the onions. Sauté until the onions are tender and the bacon is crisp. Add the vinegar, honey, and mustard. Cook, stirring, for 2 minutes. Stir in the brandy and cook for 5 minutes. Remove from the heat and cool until warm.

◆ Meanwhile, husk the corn. With a knife, cut the corn kernels from the cobs. Place the kernels in a large bowl and add the spinach and pine nuts. Pour the warm dressing over the spinach mixture and toss. Divide among serving plates. Garnish with the flowers, if desired. Cut each bread into quarters and serve with the salad.

Southwestern Salad Rolls

All your favorite Tex-Mex flavors—spicy salsa, ripe avocado, tender black beans, and pungent cilantro—are wrapped up into colorful tortilla rolls. For picnics, skip the greens and serve the rolls whole; simply wrap each in a sheet of aluminum foil and transport in a towel-lined basket to keep them warm. These handy rolls are equally delicious unbaked; in this case, wrap some salad greens into each roll for extra crunch and carry them in the cooler.

MAKES 4 SERVINGS

8 6-inch flour tortillas

1 cup chunky salsa

2 small avocados, pitted, peeled, and quartered lengthwise

¾ cup cooked black beans, rinsed and drained if canned

¼ cup finely chopped red onion

3 tablespoons chopped fresh cilantro leaves

6½ ounces Cheddar cheese, shredded (1½ cups plus 2 tablespoons)

6 cups mixed salad greens

12 fresh cilantro sprigs

¼ cup finely chopped sweet red pepper

◆ Heat the oven to 350°F. Separate the tortillas and spread them out on a flat work surface. Spread 2 tablespoons of the salsa on each.

◆ For each tortilla roll, thinly slice an avocado quarter crosswise and arrange the slices in a single layer on the salsa. Continue layering each tortilla with 1½ tablespoons black beans, 1½ teaspoons red onion, and about 1 teaspoon cilantro. Sprinkle 3 tablespoons of the cheese over each.

◆ Tightly roll up each tortilla, jelly-roll style. Place the rolled tortillas, seam side down, on a baking sheet. Bake for 12 minutes, then set aside to cool slightly.

◆ Meanwhile, divide the salad greens among 4 serving plates; scatter 3 cilantro sprigs and 1 tablespoon of sweet red pepper over each salad.

◆ With a serrated knife, cut each rolled tortilla crosswise into 5 pieces. To serve, stand 10 sliced tortilla pieces, cut side up, on each salad. Top each with some of remaining 2 tablespoons cheese and serve.

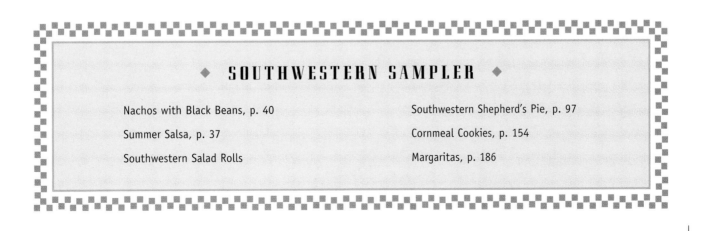

◆ SOUTHWESTERN SAMPLER ◆

Nachos with Black Beans, p. 40

Summer Salsa, p. 37

Southwestern Salad Rolls

Southwestern Shepherd's Pie, p. 97

Cornmeal Cookies, p. 154

Margaritas, p. 186

Sesame Chicken Salad

If you can't find black sesame seeds or Chinese wheat noodles in your local Asian market, use toasted white sesame seeds and vermicelli, both readily available in grocery stores. Toast the white sesame seeds in a dry skillet, stirring constantly, over medium heat for 3 minutes before adding them.

MAKES 6 SERVINGS

3 tablespoons low-sodium soy sauce

3 tablespoons vegetable oil

2 tablespoons Oriental sesame oil

2 cloves garlic, finely chopped

1 tablespoon finely chopped peeled fresh ginger

1 tablespoon rice-wine vinegar

1 teaspoon sugar

1½ pounds skinless, boneless chicken breasts, cut into ¾-inch-thick strips

Salt

1 8-ounce package dried Chinese wheat noodles

3 cups broccoli flowerettes

6 green onions

1 sweet red pepper, seeded and thinly sliced

1 sweet yellow pepper, seeded and thinly sliced

1 teaspoon cornstarch

¼ to ½ teaspoon crushed red pepper

2 teaspoons black sesame seeds

◆ In a 1-cup glass measuring cup, combine the soy sauce, 2 tablespoons of the vegetable oil, the sesame oil, garlic, ginger, vinegar, and sugar. Stir in enough water to measure 1 cup. Put the chicken into a medium-size bowl and pour half of the soy sauce mixture over it. Set aside to marinate while completing steps 2 and 3.

◆ In a 5-quart kettle or saucepot, heat 3 quarts lightly salted water to boiling, and add the noodles and broccoli flowerettes. Cook for 3 minutes, or until the noodles are al dente. Drain, rinse the noodles and broccoli briefly under cold water, and drain again. Transfer the noodles and the broccoli to a large serving bowl, and set aside.

◆ Coarsely chop the tops of the green onions and add to the bowl with the noodles. Finely chop the white part of the green onions. In a large skillet, heat the remaining 1 tablespoon vegetable oil over medium heat. Add the white part of the green onions and the red and yellow pepper slices. Sauté until the peppers are just tender—about 5 minutes. With a slotted spoon, remove the vegetables to the bowl with the noodles.

◆ In the same skillet, cook the chicken with the marinade in 2 batches, until golden brown and cooked through—6 to 7 minutes. Remove the chicken to the bowl with the noodles and vegetables.

◆ Add the cornstarch and crushed red pepper to the remaining soy sauce mixture and stir to dissolve the cornstarch. Pour the mixture into the skillet and heat to boiling, stirring constantly, until slightly thickened. Remove from the heat, add the sesame seeds, and pour over the noodles, vegetables, and chicken. Toss just until the sauce is evenly distributed. Serve immediately.

Smoked Turkey Salad with Raspberry Vinaigrette

The vinaigrette can be made a day ahead, which will allow the flavors to marry, and using store-bought turkey breast also saves time. Assemble just prior to serving to prevent the salad greens from wilting.

MAKES 4 SERVINGS

12 thin stalks (½ pound) asparagus

¼ cup olive oil

3 tablespoons raspberry vinegar

2 tablespoons fresh red raspberries

2 teaspoons sugar

⅛ teaspoon salt

4 4-ounce slices (¼ inch thick) smoked
    turkey breast

4 cups mixed salad greens

½ cup (½ half-pint basket) fresh red raspberries

Assorted dried, pesticide-free, edible flower petals
    (optional)

♦ Trim and discard the tough stems of the asparagus stalks. In a 3-quart saucepan, heat the asparagus and enough water to cover to boiling over high heat. Reduce the heat to medium and cook for 1 minute. Drain the asparagus in a colander and set aside to cool to room temperature.

♦ In a blender, combine the oil, vinegar, raspberries, sugar and salt until combined.

♦ To serve, arrange 3 stalks of asparagus side by side on each of 4 serving plates. Place one slice of turkey on top of the asparagus on each plate with 1 cup of salad greens. Divide fresh raspberries among the serving plates and sprinkle with some of the flower petals, if desired. Pulse the vinaigrette several times in the blender and pour over the salad.

♦ EDIBLES IN THE WILD ♦

You may be tempted on your stroll into the countryside to dine on edible flowers, berries, or mushrooms found along the way. Keep in mind that it is illegal to pick flowers growing in the wild—they are often native species perilously close to endangerment. Berries growing in the wild can be poisonous, so beware: Unless you are a trained forager, do not eat what you find.

You can, however, use elements in the wild to help decorate your picnic or porch. Try using things like acorns or pinecones as centerpieces. Either can be simply arranged in a bowl and set out on the table or blanket. In the fall you can collect vibrantly-colored leaves and scatter them around your blanket. For a picnic on the beach, try mixing sand with dark shells in colored plastic cups. They can also do double-duty as a weight for napkins, paper plates, or your blanket. A bowl full of crabapples not only makes a beautiful green and red centerpieces, but will give off a lovely scent.

Pepper-Crusted Filet Mignon Salad

Lay this elegant mélange of beef tenderloin, new potatoes, and roasted peppers on a bed of baby mesclun greens, if available, for a perfectly romantic porch supper worthy of your finest china. The recipe can easily be multiplied for larger parties.

MAKES 2 SERVINGS

1 large (½ pound) red potato, cut into ½-inch cubes

2 tablespoons butter

1 medium-size red onion, sliced

1 teaspoon honey

1 teaspoon cracked black pepper

¼ teaspoon ground black pepper

¼ teaspoon salt

1¾-pound 1-inch-thick piece filet mignon or 2 large
　　(6 ounces each) beef tenderloin steaks

2 cups mixed salad greens

8 endive leaves

½ 7-ounce jar roasted sweet red-peppers, drained
　　and cut into strips

◆　Place the potato cubes and enough water to cover in a 1-quart saucepan. Cover, and heat to boiling over high heat. Cook the potato cubes just until tender—about 8 minutes. Drain the potato cubes in a colander and set aside.

◆　In the same saucepan, melt 1 tablespoon of the butter over medium heat. Add the onion and sauté just until softened—3 to 5 minutes. Reduce the heat to low and stir in the honey. Cover and cook, stirring occasionally, until the onion is caramelized—about 5 minutes. Remove the onion mixture from the heat and keep warm.

◆　On waxed paper, combine the black peppers and salt and roll the filet in the pepper mixture to coat evenly. In a heavy skillet, heat the remaining 1 tablespoon butter over medium heat. Add the filet and brown well on both sides—about 4 minutes. Continue to cook to the desired doneness—3 to 5 minutes longer for medium-rare.

◆　Transfer the filet to a cutting board and let stand for 5 minutes. Meanwhile, divide the mixed salad greens between 2 plates. In the center of the salad greens place 4 endive leaves, in spoke-fashion, and top with the potato cubes. Slice the filet into 8 pieces and place one between each of the endive leaves. Place the pepper strips on top of the salad and garnish with the onion slices.

Warm Dandelion Salad with Smoked Venison

Venison is a very rich, heavy meat that is perfect for smoking. Any kind of smoking chip will work well here, but hickory or applewood will both add a note of sophistication that perfectly complements the dandelion greens.

MAKES 4 SERVINGS

1 handful hickory or applewood chips,
    soaked

1 ¾-pound venison steak (¾ inch thick)

2 tablespoons water

½ teaspoon salt

1 cup skim milk

3 tablespoons all-purpose flour

2 tablespoons sugar

⅛ teaspoon ground black pepper

3 tablespoons cider vinegar

1 pound tender, young dandelion greens,
    trimmed and washed

Pesticide-free chamomile flowers (optional)

◆ In the bottom of a 5- or 6-quart Dutch oven, place the wood chips. Place a wire rack over the chips. Sprinkle the venison with the water and ¼ teaspoon salt. Place the venison on the wire rack. Cover the Dutch oven with a tight-fitting lid and cook over medium heat until smoke starts to seep from under the lid—3 to 5 minutes. Remove from the heat and let stand for 5 minutes. Quickly remove the venison from the Dutch oven and replace the lid. Set the Dutch oven aside to cool for 30 to 45 minutes before opening so that the smoke from the wood chips doesn't escape into the house. Set the venison aside to cool slightly.

◆ In a 1-quart saucepan, combine the milk, flour, sugar, the remaining ¼ teaspoon salt, and the pepper. Cook over medium heat, stirring until the mixture thickens—3 to 5 minutes. Remove the saucepan from the heat and stir in the vinegar. Set the hot dressing aside.

◆ In a large bowl, combine the dandelion greens and ½ cup of the hot dressing. Divide the greens among 4 serving plates. Cut the venison into 20 thin slices and place 5 slices on top of each serving of greens. Garnish with the chamomile flowers, if desired.

New England Clambake Salad

All the flavors of a traditional clambake combine in this salad, cooked in a single pot. For porch suppers, layer the ingredients in a large glass bowl so all can see the colorful arrangement of potatoes, corn, lobsters, mussels, and clams. Fingerling potatoes are a yellow-fleshed variety that are about 1 inch in diameter and 2 to 4 inches long. Their waxy texture makes them a good choice for salads, but any large yellow-fleshed or smooth white-fleshed potato can be substituted; just cut each one into 2-inch pieces.

MAKES 4 SERVINGS

Lemon-Basil Dressing

1¼ cups packed fresh basil leaves

½ cup mayonnaise

3 tablespoons fresh lemon juice

1 tablespoon olive oil

1 clove garlic, chopped

¼ teaspoon sugar

¼ teaspoon ground black pepper

1 to 2 tablespoons water, as needed

Clambake Salad

1¼ pounds small red potatoes

1¼ pounds Fingerling potatoes

4 ears fresh yellow corn, shucked and silk removed

4 1-pound lobsters

12 mussels, scrubbed and beards removed

12 littleneck clams, scrubbed

2 fresh basil sprigs

◆ Prepare the lemon-basil dressing: In a food processor fitted with the chopping blade, process the basil, mayonnaise, lemon juice, oil, garlic, sugar, and pepper until smooth. Thin with the water until the mixture has the consistency of a salad dressing. Refrigerate.

◆ Fill an 8-quart saucepot with 2½ inches of water and heat to boiling. Add the potatoes and cook for 12 to 15 minutes, or until the potatoes are tender but still retain their shape. Meanwhile, cut each ear of corn into quarters and add the corn quarters to the potatoes during the last 2 minutes of cooking. With a slotted spoon or strainer, remove the potatoes and corn to a large serving bowl or platter and set aside.

◆ Drain off all but 1 inch of the cooking water and reheat to boiling. Add the lobsters to the pot, head first; cover and cook for 10 to 12 minutes, or until bright red and one small leg pulls off easily, indicating that the lobster is completely cooked. Reserving the cooking water, remove the lobsters to a colander; rinse and set aside to drain and cool.

◆ Add the mussels and clams to the simmering water remaining in the pot and cover and cook for 3 minutes, or until all the shellfish have completely opened. Drain the mussels and clams very well. Discard any that don't open. Arrange with the potatoes and corn in a large bowl or on a serving platter.

◆ Remove the claw and tail meat from all the lobsters and arrange with the vegetables and shellfish. Garnish with the basil sprigs, if desired, and serve with the lemon-basil dressing.

Crab Salad

Your family's silver teaspoons make elegant servers for this flavorful salad. However, don't feel compelled to serve them in spoons; the salad is just as lovely served on individual salad plates.

MAKES 24 APPETIZERS

¼ pound fresh crabmeat

2 tablespoons sour half-and-half

1 tablespoon fresh lemon juice

¼ teaspoon crab-boil seasoning

3 tablespoons small watercress leaves

2 teaspoons salmon caviar

◆ In a medium-size bowl, pick through the crabmeat to remove any pieces of the shell. Add the sour half-and-half, lemon juice, and crab-boil seasoning. Mix until well combined. Cover the crab salad with plastic wrap and refrigerate until ready to serve.

◆ To serve, measure 1 level teaspoon of the crab salad and place in the center of 1 silver teaspoon. Top the salad with 1 watercress leaf and 2 or 3 caviar eggs. Repeat, placing the remaining crab salad, watercress, and caviar on silver teaspoons.

◆ TAILGATE PICNIC ◆

Tailgate picnics are one of the best parts of any outing to the ballfield. The best parking always comes first-come-first-serve, so people get there early. Park the car in the shade so the food won't be in the sun. Once you have parked the car, bring out the cooler. Select things that will sit out well, Summer Salsa, p. 37, with chips, Hummus, p. 36, with carrot & celery sticks, Southwestern Salad Rolls, p. 73, Pecan-Crusted Chicken, p. 88, Turkey & Corn Fajitas, p. 93, Caramelized Onion Relish, p. 112, Steak Sandwich, p. 148, and Chocolate Chunk Cookies, p. 158.

Shrimp & Melon Salad

A dressing made of lime juice, sesame oil, and soy sauce unites melon cubes and sautéed shrimp. Serve with Pesto Focaccia, p. 134, and a bottle of white zinfandel for a refreshing meal great for a sunny day at the beach! Keep the salad cold until the last minute, and don't forget to provide plenty of cold water.

MAKES 4 SERVINGS

3 tablespoons peanut oil

1 pound large shrimp, shelled and deveined

1 tablespoon finely chopped peeled fresh
   gingerroot

2 cups (1-inch pieces) mixed melon

⅓ cup fresh lime juice

2 green onions, thinly sliced

1 tablespoon sugar

1 tablespoon sesame oil

1 tablespoon soy sauce

¼ teaspoon hot red-pepper sauce

4 leaves green-leaf lettuce

4 leaves red-leaf lettuce

◆ In a large skillet, heat 1 tablespoon peanut oil over medium heat. Add the shrimp and gingerroot. Cook, stirring occasionally, until the shrimp are pink and cooked through—4 to 5 minutes.

◆ Transfer the shrimp mixture to a large bowl. Stir in the melon pieces, lime juice, green onions, the remaining 2 tablespoons peanut oil, the sugar, sesame oil, soy sauce, and red-pepper sauce. Cover and refrigerate, stirring occasionally, until cold—at least 1 hour.

◆ To serve, arrange the lettuce around the edge of a chilled serving platter. With a slotted spoon, stir the shrimp and melon mixture and spoon into the center of the lettuce. Serve the lime-juice mixture from bowl as the dressing with the salad.

MAIN DISHES

Entrees play the starring role at dinner parties, and somehow taste even better when enjoyed amid the great outdoors. When entertaining, spend a few moments on small details to transform an ordinary get-together into an event everyone will remember. Bring out your best china, silver, and table linens. Fresh flowers, cloth napkins, and candlelight add ambiance. A garnish of fresh herb sprigs or edible flowers on each plate is the perfect finishing touch.

Pecan-Crusted Chicken

A sophisticated alternative to traditional Buffalo wings, these nutty, crunchy hors d'oeuvres are easy to transport. Pile the drumsticks in the center of a napkin-lined basket and arrange the colorful carrots and sugar-snap pea pods around them; carry the dipping sauce separately.

MAKES 4 SERVINGS

Pecan-Crusted Chicken

12 chicken drumsticks (about 3 pounds)

2 large eggs

1 tablespoon Dijon-style prepared mustard

¼ teaspoon salt

¼ teaspoon cracked black pepper

1½ cups pecans

3 slices whole-grain bread, coarsely
   torn into pieces

4 large carrots

½ pound sugar-snap pea pods

Honey-Mustard Sauce

½ cup honey

¼ cup apple or orange juice

2 tablespoons Dijon-style prepared mustard

1 tablespoon cider vinegar

◆ Heat the oven to 400°F. Lightly oil 2 rimmed baking sheets.

◆ Prepare the pecan-crusted chicken: Rinse the chicken drumsticks and pat dry. In a pie plate, beat the eggs, mustard, salt, and pepper until well mixed. In a food processor fitted with the chopping blade, process the pecans and bread until finely chopped. Pour into a 1-quart plastic food-storage bag.

◆ One at a time, roll the drumsticks in the egg mixture to coat evenly and place in the bag with the pecan mixture. Shake gently until the drumsticks are evenly coated with the pecan mixture. Arrange the drumsticks on the oiled baking sheets.

◆ Bake the chicken for 40 to 45 minutes, or until golden brown and the juices run clear when a drumstick is pierced with a fork.

◆ Meanwhile, peel the carrots and slice each one lengthwise into 4 to 6 strips. Rinse and drain the sugar-snap pea pods. Remove and discard stem ends and strings.

◆ Prepare the honey-mustard sauce: In a 1-cup glass measuring cup or small bowl, combine the honey, apple juice, mustard, and vinegar until well blended. Transfer to a serving bowl.

◆ Remove the drumsticks from the oven and transfer to a serving basket or a platter. Arrange the carrots and the sugar-snap pea pods around the drumsticks and serve with the honey-mustard sauce alongside.

TO MAKE PAPER BOOTIES

For each bootie, cut a 4-inch square from brown wrapping paper. One at a time, fold the squares in half, gently without creasing the paper at the fold. Make cuts, $\frac{1}{8}$ inch apart, through the fold, to within $\frac{3}{4}$ inch of the cut edges. To attach to drumsticks, carefully wrap the uncut ends of paper strips around the bony ends of the drumsticks and secure with some tape.

Chicken & Herb Loaf

Since it travels well, meat loaf is a perennial picnic pleaser. In this version, a garlicky mashed potato crust keeps the meat loaf moist and tender. For picnics, transport the loaf whole, wrapped tightly in aluminum foil, and slice just before serving. Carry the mushroom and herb garnishes separately in plastic containers.

MAKES 6 SERVINGS

3 large (1½ pounds) baking potatoes,
   peeled and quartered

4 slices whole-wheat bread

1 pound ground chicken

1 large egg, separated

1 teaspoon salt

½ teaspoon ground black pepper

1 10-ounce package white mushrooms

½ cup packed fresh parsley leaves

¼ cup sliced green onions

2 cloves garlic, finely chopped

2 tablespoons butter

¼ cup milk

½ pound assorted wild mushrooms (shiitake,
   Cremini, oyster)

Fresh thyme and rosemary sprigs
   for garnish

◆ In a 2-quart saucepan, heat the potatoes and enough water to cover to boiling over high heat. Reduce the heat to low, cover, and cook for 15 to 20 minutes.

◆ Meanwhile, heat the oven to 350°F. Lightly grease the center of a 12-inch ovenproof platter.

◆ In a food processor fitted with the chopping blade or with a hand-held grater, process or grate 2 of the slices of whole-wheat bread into crumbs. In a large bowl, mix together the bread crumbs, chicken, egg white, ½ teaspoon of the salt, and the pepper until well combined.

◆ In a food processor fitted with the chopping blade, process the remaining 2 slices whole-wheat bread, ½ cup of the smallest white mushrooms, the parsley, and green onions until finely chopped.

◆ On a piece of waxed paper, pat out the chicken mixture to an 8-inch square. Pat the mushroom mixture into an even layer on the chicken mixture. Roll up the mixtures jelly-roll fashion. Using waxed paper for support, lift the rolled loaf onto the greased platter, and pull the waxed paper out from underneath the loaf. Bake for 20 minutes.

◆ Meanwhile, in a small saucepan, sauté the garlic in 1 tablespoon of the butter over medium-low heat until lightly browned. Remove from the heat and stir in the milk. When the potatoes are tender, drain and discard the water. In the same saucepan, with a hand-held electric mixer on medium-low, beat the potatoes until well broken up. Beat in the remaining ½ teaspoon of the salt, half of the milk mixture, and the egg yolk. Gradually beat in half of the remaining milk mixture until the potatoes are fluffy. They won't be completely smooth because of the garlic.

◆ Remove the loaf from the oven and evenly cover with the mashed potatoes. Return to the oven and bake for 25 to 30 minutes longer or until golden brown.

◆ Meanwhile, in a large skillet, melt the remaining 1 tablespoon of the butter. Add the remaining white mushrooms and the wild mushrooms and sauté until just tender. Arrange the mushrooms around the loaf and garnish with the herb sprigs.

Chicken & Mushroom Wellington

A simple diamond pattern is an elegant touch atop these single-serving purses of golden puff pastry-cloaked chicken and portabello mushrooms, but you can use tiny cookie cutters to form other decorative shapes such as leaves or hearts. Though perfect for a romantic porch supper for two, the recipe is easily doubled or tripled for larger parties.

MAKES 2 SERVINGS

1 17¼-ounce package frozen puff pastry sheets

1 14¼-ounce can unsalted beef-flavored broth

⅓ cup red wine, preferably cabernet sauvignon

½ ounce dried porcini mushrooms

2 tablespoons butter

½ ounce finely chopped onion

1 teaspoon chopped fresh rosemary or ½ teaspoon
    dried rosemary leaves

3 cups fresh spinach, tough stems removed

½ teaspoon salt

2 4-inch-wide portabello mushrooms,
    stems removed

2 skinless, boneless chicken breast halves

1 large egg beaten with 1 tablespoon milk

1 cup mixed baby vegetables, cooked (optional)

2 fresh rosemary sprigs (optional)

♦ Thaw the pastry for 25 minutes. Meanwhile, in a 1-quart saucepan, heat the broth, wine, and porcini mushrooms to boiling over high heat. Reduce the heat to medium and simmer the mixture until it is reduced to about ⅔ cup. Strain the broth mixture into a small bowl and reserve the porcini mushrooms. Stir 1 tablespoon of the butter into the strained broth mixture and set the sauce aside. Finely chop the porcini mushrooms and set aside.

♦ In a large skillet, melt the remaining 1 tablespoon butter over medium heat. Add the onion and sauté for 5 minutes. Stir in the rosemary and cook for 1 minute. Add the spinach and ¼ teaspoon of the salt. Cover and cook for 2 minutes, or until the spinach is wilted. Remove from the heat, add the reserved porcini mushrooms, and set aside.

♦ Heat the oven to 375°F. Lightly grease a baking sheet. On a lightly floured surface, unfold 1 puff pastry sheet to a 9-inch square. With a rolling pin, roll out the pastry to a 12- by 10-inch rectangle, smoothing any creases. Cut the pastry into 3 pieces: a 12- by 3-inch strip, a 7-inch square, and a 7- by 5-inch rectangle. Repeat the rolling and cutting with the remaining puff pastry sheet.

♦ On both the 7- by 5-inch pastry rectangles, place a portabello mushroom upside down. Top each mushroom with a chicken breast half and sprinkle all the chicken breasts with the remaining ¼ teaspoon salt. Top the chicken with some of the spinach mixture. Brush some of the egg mixture on the pastry around the mushrooms. Cover the chicken-and-vegetable filling with a 7-inch pastry square. Press gently around the filling to seal the top of the pastry to the bottom of the pastry. Trim the edges to make a round. With a spatula, transfer each pastry round to the greased baking sheet.

♦ Garnish the tops of the rounds: From the remaining 12- by 3-inch pastry strips, cut eight 6-inch-long by ¼-inch-wide strips and twenty eight ½-inch diamonds. Brush the top of the round with the egg mixture. Top with the pastry strips and the diamonds arranged in alternating rows. Brush lightly with the egg mixture and bake for 25 to 30 minutes, or until the pastries are puffed and golden brown. Cool for 5 minutes.

◆ Meanwhile, reheat the sauce and divide between 2 serving plates. Place each filled pastry in the sauce and cut in half to reveal the filling. Serve with the baby vegetables and garnish with the rosemary sprigs, if desired.

Turkey & Corn Fajitas

For informal porch suppers, allow guests to assemble their own fajitas just like in a Mexican restaurant; simply lay out the warmed tortillas in a napkin-lined basket, the turkey filling and sour cream in separate bowls. Guacamole, salsa, shredded lettuce, and sliced green onions are other finishing touches worth furnishing for your fiesta. Leftover cooked chicken or shrimp can be used in place of the turkey, and the recipe is easily multiplied for bigger crowds.

MAKES 4 SERVINGS

2 teaspoons olive oil

1 medium-size onion, sliced into thin rings

1 small sweet green pepper, seeded and cut into
   thin strips

1 clove garlic, finely chopped

½ teaspoon ground cumin

1 cup chunky salsa

½ cup fresh, canned, or frozen whole-kernel corn

2 cups shredded cooked turkey

4 8-inch flour tortillas

4 tablespoons nonfat sour cream

◆ In a large skillet, heat the oil over medium heat. Add the onion and green pepper and sauté for 10 minutes. Add the garlic and cumin and sauté for 1 minute longer. Reduce the heat to low and stir in the salsa and corn. Cook, stirring occasionally, for 5 minutes. Add the turkey and cook just until heated through.

◆ Just before serving, warm the tortillas following the package directions. Divide the turkey mixture equally among the tortillas, mounding it across the middle of each. Top each serving with 1 tablespoon sour cream. Fold the sides of the tortillas over to enclose the turkey mixture, and serve immediately.

German Pancakes with Roasted Red-Pepper Chicken

These light, golden pancakes rise to great heights in the oven, then fall to make a perfect cup for a festive chicken filling.

MAKES 12 PANCAKES

½ cup chopped roasted sweet red pepper

3 tablespoons mayonnaise

1 tablespoon balsamic vinegar

¼ teaspoon ground black pepper

⅛ teaspoon salt

1 cup chopped cooked chicken

1 green onion, finely chopped

3 large eggs

⅓ cup unsifted all-purpose flour

⅓ cup milk

¼ teaspoon salt

1 tablespoon vegetable shortening, melted

◆ Set aside 2 tablespoons of the chopped red pepper. Place the remaining 2 tablespoons chopped red pepper in a food processor fitted with the chopping blade. Add the mayonnaise, vinegar, pepper, and salt; process until the mixture is pureed. Transfer to a medium-size bowl and stir in the chicken, green onion, and the reserved 2 tablespoons red pepper. Refrigerate the mixture until ready to serve.

◆ Heat the oven to 450°F. In a medium-size bowl, with an electric mixer on high speed, beat the eggs until thick and fluffy. Reduce the mixer speed to low and gradually beat in the flour, milk, and salt.

◆ Place 2 pans, each containing six 2½-inch heart-shaped molds, or a muffin pan with twelve 2½-inch cups, into the oven for 5 minutes to heat. Remove the pans from the oven and brush the cups with the melted shortening. Divide the batter among the cups and bake for 10 to 12 minutes, or until puffed and lightly browned.

◆ Remove the pancakes from the cups to a wire rack. Cool for 5 to 10 minutes, or until the centers fall, leaving a slight indentation. Spoon the chicken mixture into the centers of the pancakes and place on a serving plate. Serve immediately. If desired, the pancakes may be cooled completely before filling and served cold.

Southwestern Shepherd's Pie

A new twist on the old standby, the slightly spicy casserole filled with flavors of the Southwest is easily portable for a picnic dinner. Right from the oven, wrap it tightly with heavy-duty aluminum foil and place it in a pie carrier or a basket lined with a towel.

MAKES 8 SERVINGS

Potato Polenta

4 cups cold water

2 medium-size potatoes, peeled and finely chopped

1½ cups yellow cornmeal

¾ teaspoon salt

1½ cups milk

Shepherd's Pie

1½ pounds ground pork

1 medium-size onion, chopped

1 medium-size sweet green pepper, chopped

2 large carrots

2 14½-ounce cans Mexican-style stewed tomatoes

2 teaspoons ground coriander

2 teaspoons ground cumin

¼ teaspoon salt

1 cup frozen green peas, thawed

1 cup shredded Monterey Jack cheese with jalapeños

1 small avocado, halved, pitted, peeled,
   and thinly sliced

◆ Prepare the potato polenta: Generously grease a 3½- or 4-quart casserole and set aside. In a 4-quart saucepan, heat 2 cups of the cold water and the potatoes to boiling over high heat. Reduce the heat to low, cover and cook until the potatoes are very tender—about 10 minutes.

◆ In a 4-cup measuring cup, combine the remaining 2 cups of the cold water, the cornmeal, and the salt. Very gradually stir the cornmeal mixture into the potato mixture. Heat to boiling over medium heat, stirring constantly. Stir in the milk and return the mixture just to boiling. Reduce the heat to low, cover, and cook for 20 minutes longer, stirring occasionally.

◆ In a large skillet, sauté the pork over medium heat for 6 to 8 minutes, or until browned on all sides. Add the onion, pepper, and carrots. Cook, stirring occasionally, for 5 minutes, or until the vegetables soften slightly. Stir in the tomatoes, coriander, cumin, and salt. Reduce the heat to low and simmer for 10 minutes.

◆ Spread 2 cups of the potato polenta into the bottom and up the side to the edge of the greased casserole. Top with the pork mixture, the peas, cheese, and sliced avocado.

◆ Heat the oven to 375°F. Spoon the remaining warm polenta into a large pastry bag fitted with a large star tip. Pipe the potato polenta around the inside edge of the casserole. Pipe 5 evenly spaced lines of the potato polenta in one direction across top of mixture, then pipe 5 lines in the opposite direction.

◆ Bake the casserole for 25 to 30 minutes or until top is lightly browned. Let rest for 5 minutes before serving or immediately wrap in heavy-duty aluminum foil.

THE WELL-STOCKED HAMPER

A picnic basket should be large enough to hold all the necessities—forks, knives, spoons, serving utensils, plates, cups, napkins, salt, pepper, and sugar or artificial sweetener packets. Using small packets of condiments will make your picnic basket lighter and easier to negotiate. There are some beautiful baskets readily available at most home decorating stores, but a large backpack, canvas or sturdy straw bag work just as well.

Items to add to ensure a picnic par excellence are matches, citronella candles, a corkscrew/bottle opener, a sharp knife with a cover, and a small cutting board. Special touches might include a tablecloth, napkins, candlesticks and taper candles, napkin rings, wicker plate holders, wine glasses, wine caddy, thermos and hot cups, and if you really want to get fancy, a vase for flowers.

Bring a plastic tarp to lay underneath your blanket or tablecloth to prevent the ground moisture from ruining your perfect picnic. Have a complete first-aid kit handy and remember clean up items such as garbage bags, extra food storage bags, and wet wipes.

Pork Stew with Pepper Dumplings

Simplicity is the key to successful porch suppers, and what could be simpler than a hearty stew prepared and served in the same pan? The tender morsels of pork marry with a medley of mushrooms, winter squash, and broccoli and are then topped with savory dumplings.

MAKES 6 SERVINGS

1 tablespoon olive oil

1 10-ounce package yellow pearl onions, peeled

12 small white mushrooms

1½ pounds boneless pork loin or shoulder, cut into 1¼-inch cubes

3½ cups water

1 teaspoon salt

⅛ teaspoon ground black pepper

1 tablespoon cornstarch

1 1-pound butternut squash, peeled, halved, seeded, and cut into 1-inch cubes

1 cup unsifted all-purpose flour

1 teaspoon baking powder

¼ teaspoon cracked black pepper

¼ cup (½ stick) butter, cut into small pieces

¾ cup milk

12 broccoli flowerettes

◆ In a 9-inch cast-iron skillet, heat the oil over medium-high heat. Add 12 of the onions and the mushrooms and sauté until lightly browned—about 5 minutes. Meanwhile, chop the remaining onions and set aside. Remove the whole onions and mushrooms to a small bowl and set aside.

◆ Add the pork to the skillet and sauté, turning occasionally, until the pieces are browned on all sides. Add the chopped onions and sauté, stirring constantly, until the onions are lightly browned. Add 3 cups of the water, ½ teaspoon of the salt, and the ground pepper. Bring to a boil over high heat, reduce the heat to low, cover and cook for 45 minutes.

◆ In a 1-cup glass measuring cup or small bowl, combine the remaining ½ cup water and the cornstarch. Stir the cornstarch mixture into the pork mixture in the skillet until incorporated. Add the squash and the reserved onion and mushroom mixture. Cover and heat the stew to boiling over high heat. Reduce the heat to low and cook for 15 minutes, stirring occasionally.

◆ Meanwhile, heat the oven to 400°F. In a medium-size bowl, combine the flour, baking powder, the remaining ½ teaspoon salt, and the cracked pepper. With a pastry blender or 2 knives, cut the butter into the flour mixture until coarse crumbs form. With a serving spoon, stir the milk into the flour mixture until a soft dough forms. Spoon the dough around the edge of the skillet.

◆ Bake the stew for 15 minutes. Remove from the oven and stir the broccoli into the stew in the center of the skillet. Return the stew to the oven and bake for 5 to 10 minutes longer, or until the dumplings are browned and the broccoli is crisp-tender.

Herbed Leg of Lamb

*Dining becomes a special event when you present this leg of lamb fragrant with lavender, thyme, basil, and oregano.
Enjoy a formal Sunday afternoon dinner by including Curried-Mushroom Crêpes, p. 44, Fresh Parsley Soup, p. 55,
Spinach Salad with Bacon Dressing, p. 72, steamed asparagus, and Rose-Scented Geranium Cake, p. 167.*

MAKES 12 SERVINGS

1 teaspoon dried basil leaves

1 teaspoon dried lavender flowers or
   2 teaspoons fresh lavender flowers

½ teaspoon dried oregano leaves

¼ teaspoon dried thyme leaves

1 7- to 8-pound bone-in leg of lamb, with pelvic
   and shank bones

1 tablespoon olive oil

½ teaspoon salt

¼ teaspoon ground black pepper

1¾ cups water

1 cup dry white wine

¼ cup unsifted all-purpose flour

Pesticide-free dried lavender flowers (optional)

Pesticide-free dried lavender sprig (optional)

Fresh thyme and oregano leaves (optional)

Fresh thyme and oregano sprigs (optional)

◆ Heat the oven to 325°F. In a small bowl, combine the basil, lavender, oregano, and thyme. Set aside 1 teaspoon of the mixture.

◆ Trim the lamb fat to an ⅛-inch thickness. Place the lamb, fat side up, on a wire rack in a shallow roasting pan. Rub the surface of the lamb with the oil and sprinkle with the remaining lavender mixture, ¼ teaspoon salt, and the pepper.

◆ Roast the lamb for 1¾ to 2 hours (about 16 minutes per pound) or to an internal temperature of 145°F for medium-rare.

◆ When the lamb is done, transfer it to a serving platter and let stand for 15 minutes before carving.

◆ Meanwhile, skim off and discard all the fat from the drippings in the roasting pan. Add the water to the drippings and stir to loosen the browned bits. In a 2-quart saucepan, with a wire whisk, stir the wine into the flour until smooth. Add the drippings, the remaining ¼ teaspoon salt, and the reserved 1 teaspoon herb mixture. Heat to boiling, stirring constantly until thickened.

◆ Just before serving, sprinkle the lamb with some additional dried lavender flowers and fresh herb leaves. Garnish with the lavender and herbs, if desired. Serve accompanied by the lavender-wine sauce.

Lamb Ragout with Couscous

This slow-simmered stew is scented with Moroccan spices and served with couscous to soak up every last bit of the aromatic gravy. The ragout can be prepared the day before and reheated over medium heat; the couscous is so quick to fix it can be cooked at the last moment.

MAKES 8 SERVINGS

1 3½-pound shank half leg of lamb

1 tablespoon olive oil

1 large onion, chopped

4 cloves garlic, chopped

1 28-ounce can whole tomatoes

3¾ cups water

1 tablespoon ground coriander

1 tablespoon ground cumin

1 teaspoon salt

1 teaspoon sugar

½ teaspoon ground black pepper

½ teaspoon ground cardamom

2 bay leaves

4 large (about 1⅓ pounds) carrots, quartered
   and cut into 2½-inch-long sticks

1 20- or 19-ounce can chick-peas,
   drained and rinsed

3 large (about 2¼ pounds) zucchini, quartered
   and cut into 2½-inch-long sticks

1 10-ounce package (1½ cups) couscous

1 tablespoon grated lemon rind

1 tablespoon chopped fresh mint

1 tablespoon chopped fresh parsley leaves

Fresh mint leaves (optional)

◆ With a sharp knife, bone the lamb. Trim and discard all the fat and gristle from the lamb. Cut the lamb into 1-inch cubes.

◆ In a 5-quart Dutch oven, heat the oil over high heat. Add the lamb cubes and brown well on all sides. Transfer the lamb to a bowl.

◆ Reduce the heat to medium. Add the onion and garlic to the Dutch oven and sauté for 1 minute. Return the lamb and its juices to the Dutch oven. Add the tomatoes with their liquid, 1 cup of the water, the coriander, cumin, ½ teaspoon of the salt, the sugar, pepper, cardamom, and bay leaves. Cover, increase heat to high, and heat to boiling. Reduce the heat to low and simmer the ragout for 45 to 50 minutes, or until the lamb is tender.

◆ When the lamb is tender, stir in the carrots and chick-peas. Cover and cook for 15 minutes, or until the carrots are tender. Add the zucchini and cook for 10 minutes longer, or until the zucchini sticks soften.

◆ Meanwhile, in a 2-quart saucepan, heat the remaining 2¼ cups of the water to boiling over high heat. Stir in the remaining ½ teaspoon salt. Remove from the heat and, with a fork, stir in the couscous. Cover tightly and set aside for 5 minutes. With a fork, stir the lemon rind, mint, and parsley into the couscous.

◆ Discard the bay leaves from the lamb ragout. Ladle the lamb ragout into the center of a large shallow serving bowl. Spoon the couscous around the edge of the bowl. Garnish with the mint leaves, if desired.

Mushroom & Veal Cobbler

A flutter of tender pastry leaves tops this savory cobbler, making it perfect for autumn suppers. For other occasions, use different shaped cookie cutters for the crust, such as hearts, stars, or moons. Both the pastry and the filling can be prepared the day ahead, allowing you extra leisure time with your guests.

MAKES 6 SERVINGS

3 slices (3 ounces) thick-cut bacon, chopped

1 pound veal stew meat, cut into 1-inch cubes

1 tablespoon olive oil

1 large onion, chopped

3 carrots, sliced ½ inch thick

2 leeks, chopped

1 10-ounce package white mushrooms, chopped

¼ pound Cremini mushrooms, chopped

3 cloves garlic, chopped

1 tablespoon chopped fresh rosemary leaves or
    1 teaspoon dried rosemary leaves

1 teaspoon ground black pepper

1 teaspoon salt

3 cups plus 3 tablespoons water

1 cup unsifted all-purpose flour

1 tablespoon finely chopped mixed fresh herbs

2 teaspoons sugar

1 teaspoon baking powder

3 tablespoons butter

⅓ cup heavy cream

2 tablespoons cornstarch

1 large egg yolk beaten with 1 tablespoon milk

◆ In a 5-quart Dutch oven over medium heat, cook the bacon until it becomes browned and crisp. With a slotted spoon, transfer the bacon to a large plate and reserve.

◆ Increase the heat to high, add the veal cubes to the Dutch oven, and cook just until browned on all sides—about 4 minutes. Transfer to the plate with the bacon.

◆ Reduce the heat to medium and add the oil to the pot. Add the onion and sauté for 5 minutes. Stir in the carrots, leeks, white and Cremini mushrooms, garlic, 1 tablespoon chopped rosemary, the pepper, and ½ teaspoon of the salt. Cook, stirring, for 5 minutes. Add the reserved bacon and veal with 3 cups water. Cover and heat to boiling over high heat. Reduce the heat and simmer for 45 minutes.

◆ In a small bowl, combine the flour, 1 tablespoon herbs, the sugar, baking powder, and remaining ½ teaspoon salt. With a pastry blender or 2 knives, cut in the butter until the mixture resembles coarse crumbs. Stir in the heavy cream and mix just until blended. Gather the dough into a ball. On a lightly floured surface, roll the dough out to a ¼-inch thickness. Using a cookie cutter, cut out leaves or other shapes. Refrigerate the dough shapes.

◆ Heat the oven to 350°F. In a small bowl, combine the remaining 3 tablespoons water and the cornstarch; stir into the veal mixture. Heat to boiling, stirring, until thickened.

◆ Ladle the veal mixture into a 1½-quart casserole. Top with the dough, overlapping the shapes, allowing some space for steam to escape. Brush with the yolk mixture.

◆ Place the cobbler on a rimmed baking sheet. Bake for 30 to 35 minutes, or until the topping is golden brown. Cool the cobbler for 10 minutes on a wire rack.

Swordfish Brochettes

These skewers are great for picnics because they can be cooked ahead of time in the oven or grilled on site, and each one makes a handy single-serving. Stack the cooked brochettes in a 13- by 9-inch baking dish and wrap tightly with aluminum foil to prevent them from rolling while transporting. For a more decorative presentation, arrange them on a platter lined with lemon leaves, lettuce, or curly red cabbage.

MAKES 4 SERVINGS

¼ cup warm water

¼ teaspoon saffron threads, finely crushed

2 small red onions

¼ cup fresh lemon juice

¼ cup olive oil

2 cloves garlic, finely chopped

¼ cup chopped fresh parsley leaves

1 tablespoon chopped fresh cilantro leaves

½ teaspoon paprika

¼ teaspoon ground cumin

¼ teaspoon salt

1¼ pounds swordfish or any firm white fish steak such as halibut, cut into 1½-inch cubes

3 small lemons, cut in half (optional)

◆ About 4 hours before serving, marinate the fish: In a 1-cup glass measuring cup, combine the water and saffron. Let the saffron mixture stand for 10 minutes, or until the water turns golden.

◆ Coarsely chop 1 of the onions and set aside. Cut the remaining onion into quarters and set aside.

◆ In a medium-size bowl, whisk together the lemon juice and oil until well combined. Stir in the saffron mixture, the chopped onion, garlic, parsley, cilantro, paprika, cumin, and salt. Add the swordfish cubes and turn to coat them on all sides. Cover the mixture and refrigerate for at least 3 hours.

◆ About 1 hour before serving, heat the oven to 375°F and lightly grease a baking sheet. Thread 1 reserved onion quarter onto each of 4 long metal skewers. Thread an equal number of the swordfish cubes onto each skewer. Place the brochettes on the greased baking sheets. Bake for 16 to 20 minutes, or until the fish turns opaque and is cooked through. Place the brochettes on a serving platter and garnish with the lemon halves, if desired.

Herbed Sole with Pickled Sweet Onions

Garnished with a sprinkling of fresh herbs and baby salad greens, this is a nice, light entree to serve out on the porch on a hot summer night. Baked for just a few minutes over a bed of pickled onions, the mild fish remains moist and offers a succulent balance to the zesty onions.

MAKES 4 SERVINGS

1 tablespoon butter

2 large (1 pound) sweet onions, sliced
   into rings

¾ cup dry red wine

1 tablespoon red-wine vinegar

1 tablespoon sugar

¼ teaspoon salt

1¼ pounds sole fillets

2 teaspoons chopped fresh chives

2 teaspoons chopped fresh oregano leaves

2 teaspoons fresh thyme leaves

2 cups mesclun or mixed greens (optional)

Fresh chives and oregano sprigs (optional)

◆ In a large skillet, melt the butter over medium heat. Pour half of the butter into a custard cup and set aside.

◆ Add the onions to the skillet and cook, stirring constantly, until lightly browned. Stir in the wine, vinegar, sugar, and ⅛ teaspoon salt into the onions. Cook, stirring occasionally, for 8 to 10 minutes, or until the onions are tender and liquid has evaporated.

◆ Heat the oven to 375°F. Spoon the onions into a 13- by 9-inch baking dish, spreading evenly. Divide the sole into 4 servings and arrange on the onions. Brush the sole with the reserved ½ teaspoon of the melted butter and sprinkle with the chives, oregano, thyme, and remaining ⅛ teaspoon salt.

◆ Bake for 8 to 10 minutes, or just until the fish flakes easily. Be careful not to overcook the fish. Carefully transfer the fish and onions onto 4 warm serving plates. Garnish with the mesclun, fresh chives and oregano sprigs, if desired. Serve immediately.

VEGETABLES
&
SIDES

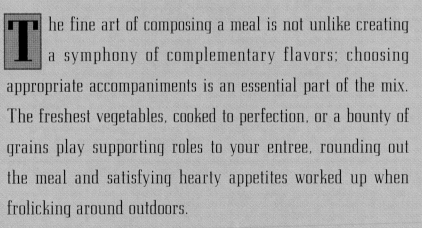

The fine art of composing a meal is not unlike creating a symphony of complementary flavors; choosing appropriate accompaniments is an essential part of the mix. The freshest vegetables, cooked to perfection, or a bounty of grains play supporting roles to your entree, rounding out the meal and satisfying hearty appetites worked up when frolicking around outdoors.

These dishes will complement any number of entrees. Choose one that balances not only the flavors of your main dish, but also the timing; many can be prepared ahead and packed-up for travel the night before.

Asian Cabbage-Herb Slaw

Coleslaw takes on a decidedly Asian twist when its spiked with cilantro, peanuts, and a refreshing lime dressing. For extra zip, add a tablespoon of rice-wine vinegar to the dressing. Since slaw tastes even better several hours after it has been prepared, it's a great addition to a make-ahead picnic spread.

MAKES 6 SERVINGS

1 tablespoon fresh lime juice

1 tablespoon olive oil

1 clove garlic, finely chopped

¼ teaspoon salt

¼ teaspoon sugar

2 cups thinly sliced savoy cabbage

1 small sweet red pepper, seeded and thinly sliced

½ cup peeled chopped cucumber

¼ cup finely chopped red onion

3 tablespoons unsalted roasted peanuts, chopped

2 tablespoons finely chopped fresh cilantro leaves

2 tablespoons finely chopped fresh mint leaves

◆ In a small container or jar with a tight-fitting lid, combine the lime juice, oil, garlic, salt, and sugar. Cover the container tightly and shake to blend the ingredients. Set the dressing aside while preparing the slaw.

◆ In a large bowl, combine the cabbage, red pepper, cucumber, red onion, peanuts, cilantro and mint. Add the lime dressing and toss well to coat the vegetables. Cover and refrigerate for at least 20 minutes before serving, stirring occasionally.

Caramelized Onion Relish

These onions, a pungent accompaniment to burgers, chicken, or fish fillets, are part of every casual meal in many families. They can be made ahead and re-heated, served at room temperature or even cold.

MAKES 6 SERVINGS

¼ cup olive oil

4 large (2 pounds) onions, thinly sliced

½ teaspoon salt (optional)

2 tablespoons balsamic vinegar

◆ In a large nonstick skillet, heat the oil over high heat. Add the onions and salt, if desired, cover, and cook for 5 minutes. Uncover the skillet and sauté the onions, stirring frequently, until they are tender and very well browned—20 to 25 minutes. Remove the skillet from the heat and stir in the vinegar. Serve hot or cold.

Asparagus Pasta

Celebrate the awakening of a new season by enjoying fresh spring asparagus with mushrooms, tomatoes, green onions, and herbs over steaming hot pasta. This dish makes the best use of shallow pasta bowls to hold every drop of the aromatic sauce.

MAKES 4 SERVINGS

⅓ cup olive oil

½ cup sliced white mushrooms

½ cup chopped green onions

4 cloves garlic, finely chopped

2 cups asparagus tips

1 cup chopped tomatoes

½ cup pitted ripe olives, quartered

½ cup dry Marsala

1 14½- or 13¾-ounce can chicken or vegetable broth

2 tablespoons cornstarch

1 tablespoon Italian seasoning blend (oregano, basil, and rosemary)

1 teaspoon ground black pepper

1 16-ounce package fusilli (curly spaghetti), cooked following the package directions

Grated Romano cheese

◆ In a large skillet, heat the oil over high heat. Add the mushrooms, green onions, and garlic. Sauté the vegetables until they are tender. Add the asparagus tips, tomatoes, and olives and cook until the tomatoes are heated through. Add the Marsala and cook the mixture until the liquid evaporates.

◆ In a small bowl, combine the chicken broth, cornstarch, Italian seasoning, and pepper until blended. Add to the vegetables in the skillet. Cook until the asparagus is tender and the sauce thickens slightly.

◆ Divide the fusilli among each of 4 pasta bowls. Spoon the vegetable mixture over the pasta and top with the Romano cheese to taste. Serve immediately.

Stuffed Artichokes Provençal

Tender artichokes filled with mushrooms, tomatoes, and pine nuts are nestled in a pool of tomato sauce, so it's best to serve them in shallow pasta bowls to allow guests to eat the leaves and neatly scoop up some sauce with every bite. Don't forget to provide empty bowls on the table for the discarded leaves.

MAKES 4 SERVINGS

4 large (1 pound each) artichokes

¼ cup fresh lemon juice

1½ teaspoons salt

2½ tablespoons olive oil

2 cups chopped onions

2 cups sliced white mushroom caps

3 cloves garlic, finely chopped

1 teaspoon dried basil leaves

1 teaspoon dried oregano leaves

1 28-ounce can whole tomatoes

4 slices fresh bread, toasted until crisp

¼ cup toasted pine nuts

1 teaspoon sugar

◆ To trim the artichokes, cut the stems off the artichokes so they will stand upright. Gently remove and discard the lowest row of leaves from the artichokes. Lay the artichokes on their sides and cut off ¾ inch from the top. With scissors, carefully snip off and discard the prickly tip of each leaf.

In a 5-quart nonaluminum saucepot, arrange the artichokes upright. (They should fit snugly in an even layer.) Sprinkle with the lemon juice and 1 teaspoon of the salt. Add enough water to cover the artichokes and heat to boiling over high heat. Reduce the heat to a simmer, cover, and cook the artichokes for 25 to 30 minutes, or until a central leaf of one artichoke comes out easily when pulled gently.

◆ Meanwhile, in a large skillet, heat 2 tablespoons of the oil over medium heat. Add 1½ cups of the onions and sauté for 5 minutes, or until light golden brown. Add the mushrooms, garlic, basil, and oregano and cook until the mushrooms soften and give up their liquid—about 5 minutes. Meanwhile, drain and reserve the liquid from the tomatoes, then seed and chop the tomatoes. Add the tomatoes and ¼ teaspoon of the remaining salt to the mushroom mixture and cook for 5 minutes. Coarsely crumble the bread. Stir the bread and the pine nuts into the mushroom mixture and remove from the heat.

◆ With a slotted spoon, remove the artichokes from the cooking liquid. Drain the artichokes upside down on a wire rack placed over a paper-towel-lined tray.

◆ In a small skillet, heat the remaining ½ tablespoon oil over medium heat. Add the remaining ½ cup onions and sauté for 5 minutes, or until light golden brown. Stir in the reserved tomato liquid, the sugar, and the remaining ¼ teaspoon salt. Cook the mixture for 5 minutes longer. In a blender or a food processor fitted with the chopping blade, puree the mixture until it is smooth. Set aside.

◆ When the artichokes are cool enough to handle, open the center cone of leaves and gently pull out the soft inner pale-green leaves to reveal the choke, or thistle, on the bottom. With a small spoon, gently scrape out and remove the choke, taking extra care to remove all of the thistle. Discard the choke.

◆ Carefully, spoon the filling into each artichoke cavity. To serve, divide the sauce among 4 serving plates, tilting the plates to spread the sauce evenly in the center. Stand each stuffed artichoke in the center of the sauce and serve. (If desired, the artichokes can be microwaved for 1 to 2 minutes to reheat.)

◆ WE EAT WITH OUR EYES ◆

Presentation marks the difference between an ordinary meal and a celebration. A little bit of ingenuity can add memorable touches to your meal, and you need not go further than the fridge to create eye-catching displays. Instead of throwing away the crown of a pineapple, slice its bottom as straight as possible and use it as a decorative centerpiece on a fruit plate, cheese platter, or appetizer tray.

With crudities, or chips with dip, try making your own serving bowl from a hollowed out round loaf of bread or red cabbage (make sure to slice a half inch off the bottom to prevent the cabbage bowl from wobbling). A trio of dips, salad dressings, or sandwich spreads can be offered in colorful bell peppers, hollowed-out onions, tomatoes, even hollow potato containers. Simply slice off the top, clean out the insides, and gently fill. Small melon halves make edible bowls for fruit salad, yogurt, or ice cream. Hollowed out seeded avocado halves is an edible dish for seafood salads.

If you are serving homemade lemon, lime, or orange sorbet for a dessert, keep the citrus rinds intact when juicing and use them as serving bowls. Cut the top third off the whole fruit and a quarter-inch slice off the bottom so it will stand up straight. Juice the fruit gently with a reamer to preserve the rind, then scoop out the remaining membranes and pulp to form a clean container. Keep the rind "bowls" in the refrigerator and fill with sorbet just before serving, or fill them in advance and keep them in the freezer until serving time.

Artichauts Chez Demery

This hearty side dish features tender baby artichokes and tiny potatoes enlivened with garlic, olive oil, and lemon juice, then roasted to perfection. This Provençal treat is equally delicious hot or at room temperature, it can be packed up for any kind of picnic.

MAKES 6 SERVINGS

6 cups water

1¼ pounds baby red potatoes

20 (1 to 1½ ounces each) baby artichokes

¼ cup fresh lemon juice

¼ cup olive oil

8 large cloves garlic, halved lengthwise

3 tablespoons chopped fresh parsley leaves

½ teaspoon salt

¼ teaspoon ground white pepper

◆ In a 5-quart nonaluminum saucepot, heat the water and potatoes to boiling over high heat. Reduce the heat to medium and cook the potatoes for 10 minutes.

◆ Meanwhile, cut each artichoke stem even with the base. Gently remove and discard the tough outer green leaves (stopping at the point where the leaves are half green and half yellow).

◆ With a slotted spoon, remove the potatoes to a colander and set aside to cool slightly. Add the artichokes and lemon juice to the same water in which the potatoes were cooked. Heat to boiling over high heat and cook for 10 minutes. Drain the artichokes well and set aside to cool slightly.

◆ Meanwhile, cut the potatoes lengthwise into quarters and cut the quarters in half crosswise. When the artichokes are cool enough to handle, cut them lengthwise into quarters. Cut out any interior leaves that are purple or pink and discard.

◆ Heat the oven to 450°F. In a large bowl, mix the potatoes, artichokes, oil, garlic, parsley, salt, and pepper. Spread the mixture in a single layer on a rimmed baking sheet and roast them on the bottom rack of the oven for 10 minutes. With a spatula, turn the mixture and roast the vegetables until lightly browned—5 to 10 minutes longer. Transfer the mixture to a serving platter and serve.

Marinated Vegetable Kabobs

This recipe makes enough for a large crowd and can be toted to picnics by stacking the kabobs in a disposable aluminum pan tightly wrapped in aluminum foil. If red pearl onions are not available—and they can be hard to find—substitute white pearl onions.

MAKES 12 SERVINGS

Vegetable Kabobs

48 white pearl onions, peeled

24 red pearl onions, peeled

1 1-pound eggplant, cut into ¾-inch cubes
    (at least 72 cubes)

2 large sweet green peppers

2 large sweet red peppers

2 large sweet yellow peppers

24 8-inch wooden skewers

Tarragon Marinade

3 tablespoons tarragon vinegar

1 tablespoon red-wine vinegar

2 teaspoons sugar

½ teaspoon salt

¼ teaspoon ground black pepper

⅓ cup olive oil

Fresh thyme sprigs (optional)

◆ Prepare the kabobs: In a 4-quart saucepan, heat 3 inches of water to boiling. Add the white and red pearl onions and cook for 5 minutes. Remove with a slotted spoon and transfer to a bowl. Set the bowl aside.

◆ Add the eggplant to the same boiling water and cook for 1½ minutes. Drain and rinse under cold water to cool slightly. Dry the eggplant with paper towels and set aside.

◆ Remove the stems and seeds from the green peppers. Cut the green peppers into quarters and cut each quarter into 4 pieces. (You will have 32 pieces of green pepper.) Repeat with the red and yellow peppers.

◆ Beginning with one piece of pepper, alternately thread 4 pieces of pepper, 3 eggplant cubes, 2 white pearl onions, and 1 red pearl onion onto each skewer.

◆ Prepare the tarragon marinade: In a small bowl, combine the vinegars, sugar, salt, and pepper. Slowly whisk in the oil.

◆ Brush the kabobs with the marinade and arrange in rows on baking sheets. Cover tightly with plastic wrap and refrigerate the kabobs for 1 hour. Reserve any remaining marinade.

◆ Heat the oven to 400°F. Remove the plastic wrap from the kabobs. Bake the kabobs for 8 minutes, or until the vegetables begin to brown on the bottom. Rotate the kabobs and bake for 7 to 8 minutes longer, or until all sides are browned and the peppers are crisp-tender.

◆ Transfer the vegetables kabobs to a platter and drizzle with any reserved tarragon marinade. Garnish the platter with the thyme sprigs, if desired. Serve immediately or cool the kabobs to room temperature and refrigerate until ready to serve.

GRILL TIPS

With their smoky flavors, grilled foods are especially delicious. Grilling means no slaving over a hot stove indoors on warm days and missing all the fun. Grilled meats, poultry, seafood, and vegetables go great with salads that can be prepared ahead of time. Always remove the old ashes from charcoal grills beforehand, and have a supply of fresh briquettes (the fast-lighting ones are convenient) and long matches.

Tools

A stiff metal brush with a notched end is essential to clean the grill before cooking (it's often easier to clean if you let the grill burn on high for a few minutes before brushing off debris).

After cleaning, lightly coat the grill or the basket with cooking oil to prevent foods from sticking. Specially designed grilling utensils have longer handles to help avoid burns. It's handy to have a grill basket with holes in it so you can cook small and delicate foods like shrimp, baby vegetables, or fish filets: They won't fall through the cracks of the grill and will be easier to handle. Always have extra oven mitts on hand. If you are an avid griller, make a carrier for grilling tools: Line a long basket with a colorful placemat. Place the grill forks, tongs, mitts, and brushes on the bottom. Keep matches in a small resealable bag with your skewers to avoid moisture.

Flavor-Additives

You may try mesquite chips, hickory chips, or bundles of dried herb branches but don't stop there. Rosemary sprigs, thyme sprigs, and bay leave branches will all provide food with a deep, aromatic flavor. They need to be soaked in water for about 20 minutes before placing them on the hot embers.

Never serve marinades from raw meat, fish, or poultry without boiling the marinade for at least five minutes to kill all the bacteria. This is best done right before serving so it keeps the food hot.

Vegetable Pizza

Loaded with a harvest of eggplant, zucchini, squash, and tomatoes over a puree of sweet red peppers—this is a knife-and-fork pizza. If you don't have a pizza paddle or a platter large enough to fit the whole pie, leave the pizza on its baking sheet so it's easy to carry to the table.

MAKES 4 TO 6 SERVINGS

1 cup unsifted all-purpose flour

1 cup unsifted whole-wheat flour

1 package rapid-rising dry yeast

½ teaspoon salt

⅔ cup very warm water (120° to 130°F.)

5 tablespoons olive oil

1 tablespoon honey

1 tablespoon cornmeal

1 7-ounce jar roasted sweet red peppers, drained

1 tablespoon white wine

½ teaspoon salt

½ teaspoon ground black pepper

1 ½-pound eggplant, cut crosswise into ½-inch-thick slices and each slice quartered

2 cloves garlic, thinly sliced

1 small zucchini, coarsely grated

1 small yellow squash, cut crosswise into ¼-inch-thick slices

1 large tomato, cut into chunks

1 teaspoon dried oregano leaves

½ teaspoon dried sage leaves, crumbled

¼ pound mozzarella cheese, shredded

Chopped fresh parsley leaves (optional)

◆ In a large bowl, combine both flours, the yeast, and salt. In a 1-cup glass measuring cup, combine the water, 1 tablespoon of the oil, and the honey and stir into the flour mixture until a soft dough forms.

◆ Turn the dough out onto a floured surface. Knead the dough, adding more flour, if necessary, until the dough is very elastic—10 to 15 minutes (the dough should be soft; do not add too much flour). Set the dough aside to rise in a warm, draft-free place until doubled.

◆ Lightly dust a large baking sheet with the cornmeal. On the baking sheet, shape the dough into a 14-inch round. Working your way around the dough, press the edge between your thumb and forefinger to create a scallop-shaped border.

◆ In a food processor fitted with the chopping blade, process the roasted red peppers, 1 tablespoon of the oil, the white wine, ¼ teaspoon of the salt, and ¼ teaspoon of the pepper until smooth. Spread the pepper mixture over the dough inside the border.

◆ In a large skillet, heat 1 tablespoon of the oil. Add the eggplant and garlic and sauté for 3 minutes, or until the eggplant is slightly tender and lightly browned.

◆ Heat the oven to 450°F. Press the zucchini into a sieve to remove the excess liquid. Place the zucchini in a medium-size bowl and toss with 1 tablespoon of the oil and spread over the pepper mixture. In the same medium-size bowl, combine the eggplant mixture, the yellow

Flavor-Additives

You may try mesquite chips, hickory chips, or bundles of dried herb branches but don't stop there. Rosemary sprigs, thyme sprigs, and bay leave branches will all provide food with a deep, aromatic flavor. They need to be soaked in water for about 20 minutes before placing them on the hot embers.

Never serve marinades from raw meat, fish, or poultry without boiling the marinade for at least five minutes to kill all the bacteria. This is best done right before serving so it keeps the food hot.

Le Tian

Summer's bounty of tomatoes, eggplant, and onions layered with melted mozzarella creates a wonderful side dish. Le Tian can be prepared ahead and refrigerated, then go straight from the oven to the table. For picnics, wrap it well in heavy-duty aluminum foil right from the oven and carry it nestled snugly in the bottom of a basket along with other warm foods.

MAKES 8 SERVINGS

4 cloves garlic, halved lengthwise

3 small (about 2 pounds) eggplants, sliced crosswise
    into ¼-inch-thick rounds

4 medium-size (about 1¾ pounds) onions,
    sliced crosswise into ¼-inch-thick rounds

6 medium-size (about 2 pounds) tomatoes,
    sliced crosswise into ¼-inch-thick rounds

3 tablespoons extra-virgin olive oil

¼ teaspoon salt

1 8-ounce package mozzarella,
    thinly sliced

2 tablespoons fresh thyme leaves

Fresh thyme sprigs (optional)

◆ Heat the oven to 400°F. Lightly oil a 12- by 9-inch oval baking dish. In the bottom of the baking dish, scatter the garlic halves. Starting at one side of the dish, create 3 lengthwise rows of vegetables that are standing on edge, alternating the slices of eggplant, onion, and tomato, until the dish is full. Brush the vegetables with 2 tablespoons of the oil and sprinkle with the salt.

◆ Bake for 45 to 55 minutes, or until the eggplant is very tender. Carefully remove the baking dish from the oven and randomly insert the cheese slices into the vegetable rows. Brush with the remaining 1 tablespoon oil and sprinkle with the thyme leaves. Return the baking dish to the oven and bake for 12 to 15 minutes, or until the cheese melts.

◆ Cool for at least 10 minutes before serving. Top with the thyme sprigs, if desired.

Grilled Vegetable Torte

Colorful layers of grilled peppers, summer squash, mushrooms, and eggplant form this smoky torte that's prepared ahead and served cold. Smaller slices of the torte can be presented as an appetizer, or offer it as a vegetarian entree alongside a whole grain salad.

MAKES 12 SERVINGS

2 ¾-pound eggplants, sliced lengthwise ⅜-inch thick

¼ cup olive oil

3 cloves garlic, finely chopped

4 large (2 pounds) sweet red peppers, seeded and quartered

3 large (1½ pounds) sweet green peppers, seeded and quartered

2 large (1 pound) sweet yellow peppers, seeded and quartered

¾ teaspoon salt

½ teaspoon ground black pepper

3 medium-size (¾ pound) portabello mushrooms, stemmed

3 medium-size (1¼ pounds) yellow squash, sliced lengthwise

3 medium-size (1¼ pounds) zucchini, sliced lengthwise

1½ cups loosely packed fresh basil leaves, coarsely chopped

2 tablespoons balsamic vinegar

◆ Heat the broiler or outdoor grill. In a 4-quart saucepan, heat 3 inches of water to boiling. Add the eggplant slices to the boiling water one at a time to prevent sticking. Return to boiling and remove from the heat. Transfer the eggplant slices to a colander and set aside to drain very well.

◆ In a small skillet, heat the oil. Add the garlic and cook just until the garlic starts to brown, immediately remove from the heat. Lightly brush both sides of the pepper quarters with the garlic oil, using about 2 tablespoons of the oil. Arrange half of the peppers on the broiler pan or grill rack. Broil 4 inches from the heat source or grill over medium-hot coals for 3 minutes. Turn the peppers and cook for 3 minutes longer or until just tender. Transfer to a large bowl and repeat with the remaining half of the peppers. Toss the cooked peppers with half of the salt and half of the pepper. Cover tightly with aluminum foil and set aside until cool enough to handle.

◆ Lightly brush both sides of the mushrooms, yellow squash, zucchini, and drained eggplant with the remaining 2 tablespoons garlic oil. Broil or grill the vegetables, one half at a time, for 3 to 4 minutes on each side, or until tender and lightly browned. Remove the vegetables to a rimmed baking sheet or roasting pan and sprinkle with the remaining half of the salt and pepper. Set aside until the vegetables are cool enough to handle.

◆ Meanwhile, with a 1½-inch star-shaped cookie cutter, cut a star from one red-pepper quarter; set the star aside and return the remainder of the red-pepper quarter to the bowl. With a sharp knife, cut out 6 yellow and 6 green pepper triangles, each measuring 4¼- by 4¼- by 2¼-inches. Set the triangles aside and return the remainder of the pepper to the bowl. Slice the mushrooms crosswise to ⅛-inch thickness.

◆ In a 9-inch springform pan, arrange half the eggplant slices in an even layer. Top with about ⅙ of the basil and about 1 teaspoon vinegar. Continue layering the vegetables, basil, and vinegar, continuing with half of the red peppers, the zucchini, the remaining half of the eggplant, the mushrooms, the remaining half of the red peppers along with all the pepper scraps, and the yellow squash. Carefully arrange the pepper triangles, alternating the green and the yellow, on top of the layered vegetables. Place the star in the center.

◆ Cover the vegetables with a sheet of waxed paper and place an 8-inch round baking pan on top. Weight it down with unopened canned products. Place the springform pan in a rimmed baking pan or tray and refrigerate it for 4 hours or overnight.

◆ Just before serving the torte, remove the cans, the 8-inch round baking pan, and the waxed paper. With a sharp knife, cut the torte into 12 wedges. Release the rim of the springform pan and allow any juices that have accumulated to drain out onto the baking pan. Carefully pour the juices into a jar and cover and refrigerate or freeze for another use. Using the pan rim as a guide to maintain the shape of torte, carefully slide the torte from the springform-pan bottom onto a serving board or plate. Carefully lift and remove the rim from the vegetable torte. Serve the torte in wedges. To pack the torte for a picnic, release the rim and pour off the juices, then refasten the rim. Wrap the torte tightly with plastic wrap and place in an insulated carrier. When ready to serve, unwrap the torte, slide it onto a serving board, and remove the pan rim. Or remove the pan rim and serve from the pan bottom.

◆ NEW NEIGHBORS ◆

Why not drop off a welcome picnic basket for neighbors just moving into your neighborhood? As we all know, moving means not knowing where any of your day-to-day items, such as pots and pans, are packed. Although your new neighbors kitchen may not be unpacked yet, after all that hard work they'd surely appreciate a home-cooked meal. Pack up a lunch of Southwestern Salad Rolls, p. 73 with an assortment of salads and chips or a supper such as Pecan-Crusted Chicken, p. 88, Asian Cabbage-Herb Slaw, p. 112, biscuits, and pickled beets. Include a selection of soft drinks and water, a batch of Chocolate Chunk Cookies, p. 158, and disposable plates, cups, utensils, and napkins. You may consider wrapping this all up in a paper tablecloth the newcomers can set their meal on. Enlist the kids help; they can make a map of the area showing where the nearest supermarket, dry cleaners, veterinary and bank are located. Top off the basket with a homemade "welcome" flag.

Spinach & Tofu Quiche

Tahini and toasted sesame seeds impart a nutty flavor to this meatless, eggless spinach pie. If you cannot find sesame oil in your local health food store, you can use peanut oil instead, but don't use Oriental sesame oil. The quiche can be served hot from the oven or at room temperature.

MAKES 8 SERVINGS

Whole-Wheat Crust

1 cup unsifted all-purpose flour

½ cup whole-wheat flour

½ teaspoon salt

⅓ cup canola or light olive oil

3 tablespoons cold water

Spinach-Tofu Filling

1 pound fresh spinach leaves (12 cups loosely packed) or 2 10-ounce packages frozen spinach, thawed and well drained

1 tablespoon sesame oil

2 cloves garlic, chopped

1 medium-size onion, chopped

1 teaspoon Worcestershire sauce or 2 to 3 drops hot red-pepper sauce

1 tablespoon cornstarch

3 tablespoons water

1 10-ounce container soft tofu, drained

2 tablespoons tahini

½ teaspoon salt

¼ teaspoon ground black pepper

⅛ teaspoon ground nutmeg

1 teaspoon sesame seeds, toasted

Sweet red-pepper strips (optional)

◆ Prepare the whole-wheat crust: Heat the oven to 400°F. In a large bowl, combine the flours, and salt. With a large spoon, stir in the oil. Add the water, a tablespoon at a time, just until the pastry holds together when lightly pressed into a ball.

◆ Between lightly floured sheets of waxed paper, roll out the pastry to a 10-inch round. Fit the pastry into a 9-inch pie plate and trim the pastry edge even with the rim of the plate. Crimp the edge of the pastry with the tines of a fork. Line the pastry with aluminum foil and fill with pie weights or uncooked dried beans. Bake the pastry for 10 minutes. Remove the pie weights and aluminum foil and set the pastry shell aside to cool.

◆ Prepare the spinach-tofu filling: If using fresh spinach, remove the tough stems from the leaves. In a 5-quart Dutch oven, heat the oil. Add the garlic and onion and sauté them until the onion is transparent. Add the Worcestershire sauce and spinach and cover the Dutch oven tightly with a lid. Cook the mixture for 2 minutes. Stir the spinach and cook, covered, for 2 minutes longer. In a small bowl, stir together the cornstarch and water. Add the cornstarch mixture to the spinach mixture. Remove the pan from the heat. Allow the spinach mixture to cool slightly.

◆ In a food processor fitted with the chopping blade, process the spinach mixture until it is coarsely chopped.

◆ Reduce the oven temperature to 375°F. In a medium-size bowl, with a fork, stir together the spinach mixture, tofu, tahini, salt, pepper, and nutmeg, Pour the filling mixture into a pastry shell.

◆ Bake the quiche for 30 minutes, or until the top is light golden brown. Sprinkle the top with toasted sesame seeds and garnish with the red-pepper strips, if desired.

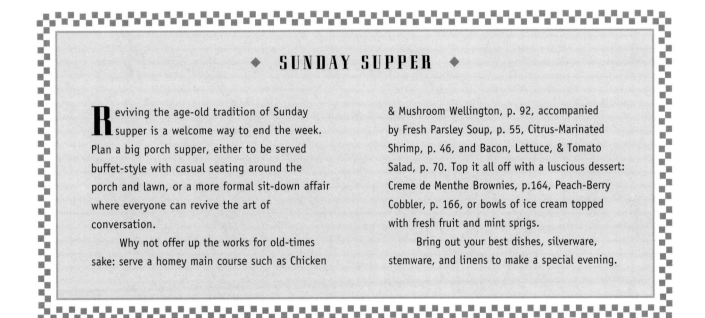

◆ SUNDAY SUPPER ◆

Reviving the age-old tradition of Sunday supper is a welcome way to end the week. Plan a big porch supper, either to be served buffet-style with casual seating around the porch and lawn, or a more formal sit-down affair where everyone can revive the art of conversation.

Why not offer up the works for old-times sake: serve a homey main course such as Chicken & Mushroom Wellington, p. 92, accompanied by Fresh Parsley Soup, p. 55, Citrus-Marinated Shrimp, p. 46, and Bacon, Lettuce, & Tomato Salad, p. 70. Top it all off with a luscious dessert: Creme de Menthe Brownies, p.164, Peach-Berry Cobbler, p. 166, or bowls of ice cream topped with fresh fruit and mint sprigs.

Bring out your best dishes, silverware, stemware, and linens to make a special evening.

BREADS
&
SANDWICHES

▲

▼

The portable nature of fragrant, crusty bread, served in
its naked glory or with any number of savory fillings,
makes it the quintessential food for outdoor entertaining.
Explore the glory of the portable meal, including quick and
hearty sandwiches from all over the country. They all just
beg to be wrapped and nestled among pillows of gingham in
a generous basket to tote to the beach, park, lake, or base-
ball game, where hungry hands will dig right in. Ingenuity
is the key here, so feel free to elaborate.

Cornsticks

The cast-iron cornstick pans you may need to invest in are well worth it for the crisp exterior and moist center of buttermilk cornsticks. Serve the sticks warm from the oven—they go nicely with egg dishes, breakfast burritos, fruit plates, chile con carne, empanadas, as well as tortilla soup.

MAKES 14 CORNSTICKS

1¼ cups unsifted all-purpose flour

¾ cup cornmeal

1 tablespoon baking powder

3 tablespoons sugar

½ teaspoon salt

1 cup buttermilk

¼ cup (½ stick) butter, melted

1 large egg

◆ Heat the oven to 425°F and generously grease 14 cast-iron cornstick molds (2 pans) with vegetable shortening. Place the pans in the oven to heat while preparing the batter.

◆ In a large bowl, combine the flour, cornmeal, baking powder, sugar, and salt.

◆ In a small bowl, beat the buttermilk, butter, and egg until well combined. Gradually add the buttermilk mixture to the flour mixture. Stir just until the dry ingredients are completely moistened (the batter will be lumpy, do not over stir.)

◆ Spoon the batter evenly into the hot greased cornstick pans. Bake the cornsticks for 10 to 15 minutes, or until the centers spring back when they are lightly pressed with a fingertip. Cool the cornsticks in the pans on a wire rack for 5 minutes. Remove the cornsticks from the pans and cool the cornsticks completely on the wire rack. Store in an airtight container.

◆ The cornsticks can be frozen, tightly wrapped, for several weeks. To reheat, defrost the cornsticks. Heat oven to 375°F. Sprinkle the cornsticks with a little water, wrap them in aluminum foil, and heat them in the oven for 5 to 10 minutes, or until they are just warmed through.

Herbed Potato-Cheese Bread

Potatoes are kneaded into the dough of rosemary-scented bread that oozes with melted cheese. Though it is satisfying enough to fill center stage for a meatless meal, you may want to cut this extraordinarily rich loaf into small wedges and serve as an appetizer or accompaniment to supper. Keep the loaf whole and tightly wrapped in aluminum foil for picnics and slice with a bread knife. Either way, provide your guests with lots of napkins.

MAKES 12 SERVINGS

1 cup plus 1 tablespoon milk

4½ to 5 cups unsifted all-purpose flour

2 packages active dry yeast

1 tablespoon sugar

1 cup mashed potatoes

½ cup (1 stick) butter, softened

1 teaspoon salt

1 pound string cheese or mozzarella

1 tablespoon fresh thyme leaves

1 teaspoon chopped fresh rosemary leaves

1 large egg

1 teaspoon poppy seeds

◆ In a small saucepan, heat 1 cup of the milk just until bubbles appear around the side of the pan. Remove from the heat, transfer to a large bowl and cool to 110° to 115°F. Add 1 cup of the flour, the yeast, and sugar. Stir the mixture until it is completely blended. Set the mixture aside for 20 minutes—the mixture will become foamy and rise.

◆ Add 3 cups of the flour, the potatoes, butter, and salt to the yeast mixture. With a wooden spoon, stir until a manageable dough is formed. Turn out onto a floured surface and knead the dough, adding the remaining flour, if necessary, until smooth and elastic—12 to 14 minutes. (The dough should be moist but not sticky.)

◆ Wash, dry, and oil the mixing bowl. Place the dough in the oiled bowl, turning to bring the oiled side up. Cover with a clean cloth and let the dough rise in a warm place, away from drafts, until doubled in size—about 1 hour.

◆ On a floured surface, roll the dough into an 18-inch round. Unravel the string cheese and pull the thick strands apart to create thinner strands. (If using mozzarella, cut it into ¼-inch cubes.) Combine the cheese with the thyme and rosemary. Mound the cheese-and-herb mixture in the center of the dough round, leaving about a 6-inch border of dough. Gently pull up the edge of the dough, bring it to the center, allowing the dough to fold in a spiral fashion, covering the cheese-and-herb mixture. Pinch the ends of the dough at the center to close the bread and create a "topknot." Transfer the bread to a large greased baking sheet. Cover with a clean cloth and let the bread rise in a warm place for 45 minutes.

◆ Heat the oven to 350°F. In a small bowl, beat together the egg and the remaining 1 tablespoon milk. Brush the top of the bread with the egg mixture and sprinkle with the poppy seeds. Bake for 55 to 60 minutes, or until golden brown and the center is firm. Cool the bread for 20 minutes on a wire rack before cutting.

Pesto Focaccia

Crisp, chewy focaccia topped with pesto and goat cheese can be served as an appetizer, or alongside a main course of Tomato Soup with Fennel, p. 55, Herbed Sole with Pickled Sweet Onions, p. 109, or Stuffed Artichokes Provençal, p. 114. Slice the focaccia into wedges while it's still warm and pile them on a colorful platter.

MAKES ONE 10 FOCACCIA

Focaccia Dough

2 to 2½ cups unsifted all-purpose flour

1 package rapid-rising dry yeast

½ teaspoon salt

⅔ cup very warm (120° to 130°F.) water

1 tablespoon olive oil

1 tablespoon honey

Pesto

½ cup tightly packed fresh basil leaves

2 tablespoons coarsely chopped walnuts

1 clove garlic

⅛ teaspoon salt

⅓ cup olive oil

2 teaspoons cornmeal

1 ounce goat cheese, coarsely crumbled

1 tablespoon pine nuts

◆ Prepare the focaccia dough: In a large bowl, combine 2 cups of the flour, the yeast, and salt. In a 1-cup glass measuring cup, combine the water, oil, and honey. Stir the water mixture into the flour mixture until a soft dough forms.

◆ Turn the dough out onto a floured surface. Knead the dough, adding some of the remaining ½ cup flour if necessary, until the dough is very elastic—10 to 15 minutes. (The dough should be soft; do not add too much flour.)

◆ Wash, dry, and lightly oil the mixing bowl. Place the dough in the oiled bowl, turning to bring the oiled side up. Cover with a clean cloth and let the dough rise in a warm place, away from drafts, until doubled in size—30 to 45 minutes.

◆ Meanwhile, prepare the pesto: In a food processor fitted with the chopping blade, process the basil, walnuts, garlic, and salt until the basil is finely chopped. With the processor running, slowly pour in the oil until the mixture has combined to make pesto.

◆ Heat the oven to 450°F. Shape the dough into a 10-inch round. Lightly dust a baking sheet with the cornmeal. Place the dough round on a baking sheet. Brush the top of the round with some of the pesto. Sprinkle with the goat cheese and pine nuts.

◆ Bake the focaccia on the middle oven rack for 10 to 12 minutes, or until golden brown. Serve, accompanied by any remaining pesto, if desired, for dipping.

Vegetable-Stuffed Whole-Wheat "Handwiches"

Freshly baked whole-wheat bread cones are filled with vegetables and drizzled with tangy honey-mustard dressing. Your favorite vegetables can be substituted for the ones suggested here. These unique bread cone molds can be purchased in cookware shops.

MAKES 8 SERVINGS

Whole-Wheat Bread Cones

1 cup milk

1 package active dry yeast

3 tablespoons sugar

3 tablespoons butter, melted

1 cup whole-wheat flour

1½ to 2 cups unsifted all-purpose flour

½ teaspoon salt

1 large egg

1 tablespoon water

Honey-Mustard Dressing

3 tablespoons cider vinegar

1 tablespoon fresh lemon juice

2 teaspoons honey

2 teaspoons water

1½ teaspoons prepared mustard

¼ teaspoon dried oregano leaves

⅛ teaspoon salt

⅛ teaspoon ground black pepper

⅓ cup olive oil

Vegetable Filling

2 medium-size tomatoes, chopped

1 cup thinly sliced green cabbage

1 cup thinly sliced red cabbage

½ cup grated carrots

½ cup chopped sweet green pepper

½ cup toasted chopped walnuts

⅓ cup chopped pitted ripe olives

¼ cup thinly sliced onion

Skewers

8 cherry tomatoes

8 small dill pickles

8 large ripe olives, pitted

8 small green lettuce leaves

◆ Several hours or the day before serving, prepare the whole-wheat bread cones: In a small saucepan, heat the milk until bubbles form around the side of the pan. Pour the milk into a large bowl and set aside to cool to 110° to 115°F. Stir in the yeast and 1 tablespoon of the sugar. Let the mixture stand until it is foamy—5 minutes.

◆ Add the remaining 2 tablespoons sugar, the butter, whole-wheat flour, 1 cup of the all-purpose flour, if necessary, and salt to make the dough manageable.

◆ Turn the dough out onto a lightly floured surface. Knead the dough, adding more flour if necessary, until it is smooth and elastic—8 minutes.

◆ Wash, dry, and lightly oil the mixing bowl. Place the dough in the oiled bowl, turning to bring the oiled side up. Cover with a clean cotton cloth and let the dough rise in a warm place, away from drafts, until doubled in size—about 1 hour.

◆ With a floured rolling pin, roll the dough to an 18- by 12-inch rectangle. Cut the dough into eight 1½- by 18-inch strips.

◆ Grease 2 baking sheets and the outside of 8 metal cream-roll cone molds. Starting at the pointed end of 1 mold, begin wrapping a strip of dough around the mold in a spiral fashion, overlapping each turn by ¼ inch. Pinch the dough together at the pointed end to seal. Stop the spiral ¼ inch from the top of the mold to allow the bread to expand. Place the dough-wrapped mold on 1 of the greased baking sheets. Repeat with the remaining strips of dough, placing 4 molds on each baking sheet. Cover with a clean cloth and let rise in a warm place, away from drafts, for 30 minutes.

◆ Heat the oven to 350°F. In a small bowl, beat the egg with the water to make an egg wash. Carefully brush the sides and tops of the dough-wrapped molds with the egg wash. Bake for 18 to 20 minutes, or until golden brown. Remove from the baking sheets and cool on wire racks for 5 minutes. With a clean cloth to protect your hands, gently pull the metal mold from the bread cones. Cool the cones completely on the wire racks. Wrap the cones in plastic food-storage bags and store in the refrigerator or freezer. Warm the cones in the oven before serving.

◆ Prepare the honey-mustard dressing: In a small bowl, with a wire whisk, combine the vinegar, lemon juice, honey, water, mustard, oregano, salt, and pepper. Slowly beat in the oil until the mixture is well combined. Serve or cover with plastic wrap and refrigerate until ready to serve.

◆ Just before serving, prepare the vegetable filling: In a large bowl, combine the tomatoes, cabbages, carrots, pepper, walnuts, olives, and onion.

◆ Prepare the skewers: Thread the tomatoes, pickles, and olives alternately onto 8 pre-soaked bamboo skewers, starting with the tomatoes and ending with the olives.

◆ To assemble the handwiches, fill each bread cone halfway with the vegetable filling and drizzle 1 teaspoon honey-mustard dressing over the filling in each cone. Stuff the cones with the remaining vegetable filling. Decoratively place a lettuce leaf in each, top with the remaining dressing, and serve with the skewered tomatoes, pickles, and olives. For picnics, wrap each handwich in aluminum foil and place the skewers in a separate container.

Polenta & Eggplant Sandwich

Unlike traditional sandwiches, these squares of parmesan-crusted creamy polenta are layered with spicy tomato-eggplant filling. They cannot be eaten out of hand, so offer forks and knives at each place setting. To free up time before your party, the eggplant mixture can be made ahead, refrigerated, and brought back to room temperature before serving.

MAKES 4 SERVINGS

3½ cups water

2 cups milk

1½ cups yellow cornmeal

½ teaspoon salt

2 tablespoons olive oil

1 small onion, finely chopped

1 stalk celery, chopped

½ cup chopped sweet green pepper

2 cloves garlic, finely chopped

1 teaspoon dried basil leaves

¼ teaspoon crushed red pepper

1 1-pound eggplant, cut into ½-inch cubes

1 14½-ounce can diced tomatoes

¼ cup red wine or water

½ teaspoon sugar

1 tablespoon chopped fresh parsley leaves

½ cup grated Parmesan cheese

2 cups mesclun or mixed greens (optional)

◆ Several hours or a day ahead, butter the bottom and halfway up the sides of two 9-inch square baking pans. In a 2½-quart saucepan, heat the water to boiling over high heat. Meanwhile, in a medium-size bowl, with a wooden spoon, combine the milk, cornmeal, and salt until blended. Slowly stir the cornmeal mixture into the boiling water. Reduce the heat to medium and cook, stirring frequently, until the mixture is very thick and mounds when dropped from a spoon—about 8 minutes. Divide the polenta between the greased pans, tilting each pan to spread the mixture evenly. Set aside to cool. Cover each pan with plastic wrap and refrigerate until firm—about 2 hours or overnight.

◆ In a large skillet, heat the oil over medium heat. Add the onion, celery, and green pepper. Sauté the mixture for 3 minutes. Stir in the garlic, basil, and red pepper and sauté for 1 minute. Add the eggplant and cook, stirring occasionally, for 5 minutes. Stir in the tomatoes with their liquid, the red wine, and sugar. Cover the skillet and cook over medium-low heat, stirring occasionally, for 30 minutes. Remove from the heat and stir in the parsley. Cool the eggplant mixture to room temperature.

◆ Just before serving, heat the broiler. With a knife, loosen the polenta around the inside edge of each pan. Invert each pan onto a baking sheet and gently unmold the polenta. Top each polenta square with ¼ cup of the grated Parmesan cheese. Broil just until the cheese melts and browns lightly.

◆ To serve, cut each polenta square into 4 squares. Place 1 square on each of 4 serving plates. Top with the eggplant filling. Cover the filling with another polenta square, creating 4 sandwiches. Cut the sandwiches diagonally in half, garnish each plate with ½ cup mesclun, if desired, and serve.

Santa Fe Chicken Sandwich

Beets, cornmeal-coated chicken, and a tangy fat-free dressing are wrapped up in tortillas for a lunch-on-the-go. Fold a festive paper napkin around each sandwich and pile them up on a pretty platter or roll each in a piece of brown kraft paper and cradle them in a handled basket. Either way, they are best served warm.

MAKES 6 SANDWICHES

1 beet (about ½ pound)

Tangy Cilantro Dressing

¼ cup nonfat sour cream

1 tablespoon fresh lime juice

1 tablespoon chopped fresh cilantro

½ teaspoon sugar

¼ teaspoon ground cumin

⅛ teaspoon chili powder

Cornmeal-Coated Chicken

1 cup yellow cornmeal

¼ cup unsifted all-purpose flour

½ teaspoon salt

1¼ cups buttermilk

1¼ pounds skinless, boneless chicken breasts, sliced into ¾-inch strips

Vegetable oil, for frying

6 10-inch flour tortillas, warmed

1 bunch (about ¼ pound) arugula, stems removed

1 small bunch (about ¼ pound) Lollo Rosso or other curly red-leaf lettuce

6 long fresh chives

◆ In a 1-quart microwave-safe bowl, place the beet in 1 inch of water. Microwave on high (100 percent) for 5 minutes. Turn the beet upside down and microwave on high (100 percent) for 5 more minutes. Remove the dish from the microwave and let cool for 10 minutes. Drain the beet and let it cool completely. Peel the beet, and cut it into ¼-inch strips. Set the strips aside.

◆ Prepare the tangy cilantro dressing: In a small bowl, combine the ¼ cup buttermilk, the sour cream, lime juice, cilantro, sugar, cumin, and chili powder. Refrigerate the dressing until ready to serve.

◆ Prepare the cornmeal-coated chicken: In a small bowl, combine the cornmeal, flour, and salt. Pour the remaining 1 cup buttermilk into a small shallow bowl. Place a few strips of the chicken into the buttermilk, coating the chicken completely. Transfer the chicken strips to the cornmeal-flour mixture, dredging them until the pieces are completely coated. Transfer to a plate and repeat the process until all the chicken is coated. Refrigerate the chicken for 10 minutes.

◆ Meanwhile, in a large skillet, heat about 1 inch of oil to 350°F on a deep-fat thermometer. When the oil is hot, place as many chicken strips into it as will fit in a single layer. When the underside of the chicken strips have browned slightly, turn and continue to cook until the other sides are browned and the chicken is done—about 4 to 6 minutes longer. With tongs or a slotted spatula, remove the chicken strips from the oil and drain on paper towels. Keep the chicken warm in a 200°F oven until ready to serve. Repeat until all the chicken pieces have been cooked.

◆ To assemble the sandwiches, place a tortilla on a serving plate. In the center of the tortilla, spoon 1 heaping tablespoon of the buttermilk-dressing. Place some of the arugula and Lollo Rosso leaves on the top of the dressing. Add 4 or 5 chicken strips and a few pieces of the beet to the greens. Fold the bottom half of the tortilla up to cover half of the ingredients, then fold the sides of the tortilla toward the center. Fold the last half of the tortilla over the filling. Carefully encircle the tortilla with a long chive and tie into a bow to secure the sandwich. Place the sandwich on a serving platter. Repeat with the remaining ingredients. Serve the remaining dressing alongside the sandwiches.

Italian Deli Roll

For a picnic, wrap the uncut roll in heavy-duty aluminum foil and surround it with a towel to retain heat. Bring along a cutting board and serrated knife to slice it just before serving (and use the board as a serving platter).

MAKES 4 SERVINGS

1 tablespoon cornmeal

Focaccia Dough, p. 134

⅛ pound sliced salami, coarsely chopped

¼ pound sliced provolone cheese,
    coarsely chopped

⅛ pound sliced pepperoni, coarsely chopped

1 7-ounce jar roasted sweet red peppers, drained
    and coarsely chopped

2 teaspoons olive oil

¼ teaspoon dried oregano leaves

◆ Heat the oven to 400°F. Lightly dust a jelly-roll pan with the cornmeal. With a rolling pin, roll out the focaccia dough to an 18- by 12-inch rectangle. Spread the salami, provolone, pepperoni, and red peppers over the rectangle, leaving a ½-inch border around the edges. Starting at one short edge, roll up the dough, jelly-roll fashion. Secure the ends and the remaining short edge by pinching the dough together between your fingers. Place the roll, seam side down, on the prepared jelly-roll pan. Brush with the oil and sprinkle with the oregano.

◆ Bake the roll for 18 to 20 minutes, or until golden brown. Cool on a wire rack for 5 minutes. Slice the roll and serve immediately, or wrap in heavy-duty aluminum foil for a picnic.

Barbecued Pork on Corn Bread

For a meal reminiscent of the deep South, heap tender pork on squares of corn bread with a side of pickled okra. Offer plenty of cheerful gingham napkins with these finger-licking treats. If you are toting this along on a picnic, carry the ingredients separately and assemble at the last minute so the corn bread doesn't become soggy.

MAKES 4 SERVINGS

Pickled Okra

2 cups water

½ cup cider vinegar

⅓ cup sugar

6 whole cloves

1 teaspoon salt

½ teaspoon *each* cumin seeds, celery seeds
   and crushed red pepper

½ pound fresh okra

Barbecued Pork

½ tablespoon vegetable oil

1 1½-pound boneless pork loin, thinly sliced

½ cup cubed (¼-inch) smoked sausage

1 medium-size onion, chopped

2 cloves garlic, chopped

1 15-ounce can tomato sauce

2 tablespoons red-wine vinegar

1 tablespoon dark molasses

1 teaspoon *each* grated peeled fresh ginger, chili
   powder, hot red-pepper sauce, ground cinnamon

Pinch of ground cloves

Chili-Corn Bread

1 cup unsifted all-purpose flour

⅔ cup yellow cornmeal

¼ cup sugar

½ teaspoon *each* baking powder, baking soda and salt

1 cup buttermilk, warmed

½ cup (1 stick) butter, melted

1 large egg

1 cup fresh or thawed frozen whole-kernel corn

½ cup finely chopped sweet green pepper

1 tablespoon canned green chilies, chopped

◆ Prepare the pickled okra at least one day in advance: In a 2-quart saucepan, heat the water, vinegar, sugar, cloves, salt, cumin seeds, celery seeds, and red pepper to boiling. Add the okra and boil for 3 minutes. Remove the pan from the heat and cool the mixture to room temperature. Transfer the okra and pickling liquid to a jar or container and cover. Refrigerate the mixture for several hours before serving.

◆ Prepare the barbecued pork: In a large skillet, heat the oil. Add half of the pork and sauté until it is lightly browned. Transfer the pork to a bowl, and repeat with the remaining pork.

◆ Add the sausage, onion, and garlic to the same skillet and cook until the onion is lightly browned. Add the tomato sauce, vinegar, molasses, ginger, chili powder, pepper sauce, cinnamon, cloves, and pork to the skillet. Heat to boiling over medium-high heat. Reduce the heat to low and cook, covered, for 45 to 50 minutes, or until the pork is tender.

◆ Meanwhile, prepare the chili-corn bread: Heat the oven to 350°F. Grease a 9-inch-round baking pan. In a large bowl, combine the flour, cornmeal, sugar, baking powder, baking soda, and salt. In a small bowl, combine the buttermilk, butter, and egg. Stir the milk mixture into the flour mixture just until combined. Gently fold the corn, chopped pepper, and chilies into the batter.

◆ Spoon the batter into the greased pan and bake for 40 to 45 minutes, or until the center springs back when lightly pressed with a fingertip. Cool the corn bread in the pan on a wire rack for 15 minutes. Remove from the pan.

◆ Just before serving, cut the corn bread into 4 wedges. Split each wedge in half horizontally. Place the bottom halves on 4 plates. Top with the pork and place the tops of the corn bread on the pork. Serve with the pickled okra.

Hot Roast Beef Sandwich

Sautéed flank steak is smothered with a hearty red-wine sauce and served on thick slices of bread for a decadent meal.

MAKES 4 SERVINGS

1 1½-pound flank steak

¼ teaspoon salt

⅛ teaspoon ground black pepper

1 clove garlic, finely chopped

1 tablespoon butter

1 10½-ounce can condensed beef broth, undiluted

1 cup dry red wine or water

3 tablespoons all-purpose flour

1 teaspoon Worcestershire sauce

8 slices thick-cut, firm white bread

◆ Place the flank steak on waxed paper. Sprinkle both sides with the salt, pepper, and garlic. In a very large skillet, over medium heat, melt the butter. Sauté the steak on one side until browned—about 5 minutes. Turn the steak and sauté on the other side until browned and the meat is the desired doneness—3 to 5 minutes longer. Remove the steak to a platter.

◆ In a small bowl, beat the beef broth into the flour until smooth. Add to the skillet along with the red wine and Worcestershire sauce. Heat to boiling, stirring constantly, until the gravy is thickened.

◆ Carve the beef into thin diagonal slices. Place 4 slices of bread on 4 serving plates. Divide the beef onto the bread and top with the remaining bread slices. Stir any beef drippings on the platter into the gravy in the skillet. Spoon the gravy over the sandwiches and serve.

Brisket & Frizzled Leeks on Corn Bread

Considered the best barbecue ever by many connoisseurs, brisket of beef is slow-cooked in garlicky sauce until it's nearly falling apart, then served on a bed of corn bread with a crunchy garnish of frizzled leeks. Brisket improves with time, so the meat can be cooked the day before serving, refrigerated, sliced, and reheated in the sauce over a medium flame.

MAKES 8 SERVINGS

Brisket

1 12-ounce bottle chili sauce

1 8-ounce can tomato sauce

½ cup light molasses

¼ cup light corn syrup

¼ cup white-wine vinegar

2 tablespoons light soy sauce

1 tablespoon olive oil

2 medium-size onions, coarsely chopped

4 cloves garlic, chopped

1 4-pound beef brisket, trimmed of excess fat

Buttermilk Corn Bread

¾ cup unsifted all-purpose flour

¾ cup yellow cornmeal

2 tablespoons sugar

½ teaspoon baking powder

½ teaspoon baking soda

½ teaspoon salt

6 tablespoons (¾ stick) butter

1 cup buttermilk

1 large egg

Frizzled Leeks

2 1-inch-thick leeks

½ cup flour

¼ teaspoon salt

¼ teaspoon ground black pepper

Vegetable oil, for frying

◆ Prepare the brisket: In a large bowl, combine the chili sauce, tomato sauce, molasses, corn syrup, vinegar, and soy sauce. In a heavy-bottomed 8-quart saucepot, heat the olive oil over medium heat. Add the onions and sauté for 5 minutes, or until light golden brown. Stir in the garlic and cook for 1 minute. Place the brisket on the onion mixture. Add the chili-sauce mixture and enough water to cover the meat. Heat to boiling over medium-high heat. Reduce the heat to low, cover, and simmer for 2 hours.

◆ Meanwhile, make the buttermilk corn-bread: Heat the oven to 350°F. Grease a 13- by 9-inch baking pan. In a large bowl, combine the flour, cornmeal, sugar, baking powder, baking soda, and salt. In a 1-quart saucepan over low heat, melt the butter; remove from the heat. Stir the buttermilk and egg into the batter until well mixed. Stir the buttermilk mixture into the flour mixture just until combined. Spread the batter into the greased pan and bake for 25 to 30 minutes, or until a cake tester inserted in the center comes out clean. Cool the corn bread in the pan on a wire rack for 15 minutes. Remove the corn bread from the pan and cool completely on the wire rack.

◆ Uncover the brisket and simmer, stirring occasionally, until fork-tender—about 1½ to 2 hours longer. Remove the brisket to a cutting board to cool. Heat the sauce remaining in the pot to boiling over high heat. Boil the sauce until it is reduced to 3 cups. Skim off the fat and reserve the sauce in a saucepot.

◆ Prepare the frizzled leeks: Cut off and discard the root ends of the leeks. Cut off and discard the dark-green leaves, leaving the bottom white portion with some light-green leaves. Cut the leeks in half lengthwise and crosswise. Then thinly slice the leeks lengthwise into julienne strips. Place the strips in a colander and rinse well under cold running water to remove any dirt.

◆ In a 1-quart saucepan, heat 1½ inches of water to boiling over high heat. Add the julienned leeks and cook for 1 minute. Drain the leeks well in a colander and then spread on paper towels to dry. In a small bowl, combine the flour, salt, and pepper. Set the flour mixture aside.

◆ Just before serving, in a large skillet, heat ½ inch vegetable oil over high heat. Add half of the leeks to the flour mixture and toss to coat lightly. Place the floured leeks in the hot oil and fry just until crisp—about 30 seconds. Remove the leeks and drain on paper towels. Repeat with the remaining leeks.

◆ To serve, thinly slice the brisket across the grain. Place the slices into the sauce in the pot. Cut the corn bread into quarters and cut each quarter diagonally to create 8 triangular pieces. Place 1 piece of corn bread on each serving plate. Arrange slices of the brisket on the corn bread and top with some of the sauce. Top each plate with the frizzled leeks and serve immediately.

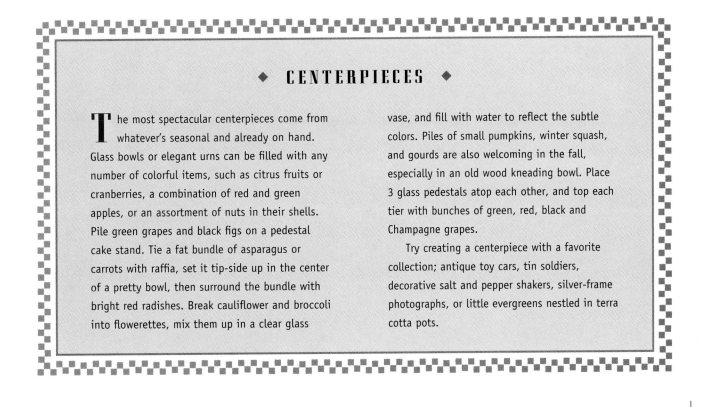

◆ CENTERPIECES ◆

The most spectacular centerpieces come from whatever's seasonal and already on hand. Glass bowls or elegant urns can be filled with any number of colorful items, such as citrus fruits or cranberries, a combination of red and green apples, or an assortment of nuts in their shells. Pile green grapes and black figs on a pedestal cake stand. Tie a fat bundle of asparagus or carrots with raffia, set it tip-side up in the center of a pretty bowl, then surround the bundle with bright red radishes. Break cauliflower and broccoli into flowerettes, mix them up in a clear glass vase, and fill with water to reflect the subtle colors. Piles of small pumpkins, winter squash, and gourds are also welcoming in the fall, especially in an old wood kneading bowl. Place 3 glass pedestals atop each other, and top each tier with bunches of green, red, black and Champagne grapes.

Try creating a centerpiece with a favorite collection; antique toy cars, tin soldiers, decorative salt and pepper shakers, silver-frame photographs, or little evergreens nestled in terra cotta pots.

ALLOWING FOR NATURE

When dining alfresco, be prepared for exposure to sun and insects. On sunny days, everyone should apply sunblock—SPF 30 is the safest and most highly recommended—and re-apply it every 3 to 4 hours.

Set your picnic up near trees. Providing umbrellas for shade is welcome on picnics or in the backyard. If you don't have umbrellas, try tacking a light, colorful sheet or blanket between two trees. Donning hats with large brims also protects from the sun. Sun and wind dehydrate skin, so it's advisable to moisturize your face and body after spending time outdoors. Insect repellent is also important; have some on hand just in case it's particularly buggy out. Mosquitoes and biting flies are repelled by citronella as well as pennyroyal. You can make your own natural insect repellent by diluting a few drops of the essential oil of either herb in a pint-sized spray bottle filled with water. Shake well and spray over exposed skin. For faces, spray the mixture into the palm of your hand and gently rub onto your face (avoid eyes when applying).

Steak Sandwich

For a shortcut version, use leftover sliced steak or even deli roast beef, as well as jarred roasted peppers.

MAKES 4 SERVINGS

1 1½-inch-thick (1 pound) well-trimmed boneless top loin beef steak

½ teaspoon salt

¼ teaspoon ground white pepper

2 large (1 pound) sweet red peppers, quartered lengthwise and seeded

1 8-ounce container fat-free sour cream

¼ cup hot-flavored prepared horseradish

2 tablespoons chopped fresh basil leaves

2 tablespoons milk

4 sesame sandwich rolls

16 large fresh basil leaves

◆ Heat the oven to 425°F. Sprinkle the steak on both sides with ¼ teaspoon of the salt and the white pepper. Arrange the steak and red-pepper quarters on a wire rack in a shallow roasting pan.

◆ Roast the steak and peppers for 12 minutes, or until the internal temperature of the steak reaches 140°F on a meat thermometer. Remove the roasting pan from the oven and place the steak on a piece of aluminum foil. Cool to room temperature on the wire rack. Wrap tightly and refrigerate until cold—about 1 hour. Transfer the red peppers to a paper bag, close tightly, and set aside. When the peppers are cool enough to handle, peel off and discard the skin. Wrap and refrigerate the peppers until ready to assemble the sandwiches.

◆ Meanwhile, prepare the horseradish sauce: In a small bowl, combine the sour cream, horseradish, chopped basil, milk, and the remaining ¼ teaspoon salt. Cover and refrigerate until ready to serve.

◆ Just before serving, on a cutting board, with a very sharp knife, thinly slice the steak. Open the 4 rolls and divide the steak among the bottoms of the rolls. Top each with 2 tablespoons of the horseradish sauce, 2 pieces of the red pepper, and 4 large basil leaves. Close the rolls and serve with the remaining sauce.

Oyster Po'Boy

These sensational sandwiches feature crunchy cornmeal-coated oysters nestled on a bed of lettuce and tomatoes. They can either be assembled on the scene by transporting each ingredient wrapped separately, or arrange the completed sandwiches in a napkin-lined basket covered with an additional napkin until serving. If large oysters are not available, pat together two small oysters between your hands to create one "large" one.

MAKES 2 SERVINGS

Tartar Sauce

½ cup reduced-calorie mayonnaise

2 tablespoons sweet pickle relish

1 tablespoon fresh lemon juice

¼ teaspoon hot red-pepper sauce

Cornmeal-Coated Oysters

⅓ cup unsifted all-purpose flour

½ cup yellow cornmeal

¼ teaspoon salt

1 large egg

6 large oysters (about ½ pint), shucked
   and drained well

2 tablespoons butter

2 7-inch club rolls

1 large tomato, cut crosswise into 6 thin slices

¼ cup shredded lettuce

1 lemon, quartered (optional)

◆ Prepare the tartar sauce: In a small bowl, combine the mayonnaise, relish, lemon juice, and red-pepper sauce until well mixed. Refrigerate until ready to serve.

◆ Prepare the cornmeal-coated oysters: On a sheet of waxed paper, spread out the flour. On another sheet of waxed paper, combine the cornmeal and salt. In a medium-size bowl, lightly beat the egg. Roll the oysters in the flour, coating each one well. Place the floured oysters in the egg and turn them several times to coat completely. Roll the oysters in the cornmeal mixture, coating them evenly.

◆ In a large skillet, melt the butter over medium heat. Add the oysters and fry for 1 to 2 minutes on each side, or until lightly browned.

◆ To assemble the sandwiches: With a serrated knife, cut the club rolls horizontally in half. Cover the bottom halves of the rolls with the tomato slices. Place 3 oysters on each sandwich on the tomatoes. Spoon 2 tablespoons of the sauce over each sandwich and top with the lettuce. Cover with the tops of the rolls. Serve with the remaining sauce on the side and a wedge of lemon, if desired.

DESSERTS

Whether it's a sensuously sinful chocolate cake or meltingly sublime fruit tart, dessert is the pièce de résistance, the grand finale to top everything off and signal the close of a meal. A blissful bite of something sweet satisfies the soul and reflects the meal. Choose from this collection of cookies, tarts, cobblers and cakes to dazzle the eye as well as the palate. Add a sprinkle of confectioners' sugar, a dollop of whipped cream, or a flutter of candied violets to each serving.

Pistachio Biscotti

These crisp cookies travel well, and make great gifts when packed in pretty tins. Try adding dried fruits—cranberries and blackberries especially—and substituting different kinds of nuts for the pistachios.

MAKES ABOUT 40 BISCOTTI

1½ cups unsifted all-purpose flour

½ teaspoon baking powder

⅓ cup shelled unsalted pistachios, coarsely
    chopped

4 large egg whites

1 large egg

¾ cup sugar

1 teaspoon vanilla extract

◆ Heat the oven to 350°F. Lightly grease 2 baking sheets. In a small bowl, combine the flour, baking powder, and pistachios. In a large bowl, with an electric mixer on high speed, beat the egg whites and egg until frothy. Gradually beat in the sugar and vanilla until very thick and pale yellow—about 5 minutes. Fold the flour mixture into the egg batter until well combined.

◆ Spoon half of the batter into a 12- by 4-inch strip on 1 greased baking sheet. Repeat on the other greased baking sheet with the remaining half of the batter.

◆ Bake the strips for 15 to 20 minutes, or until light golden brown. Cool on the baking sheets on wire racks for 10 minutes. Remove the strips from the baking sheets and cut crosswise into ½-inch-thick slices. Place a single layer of the biscotti on the same baking sheets, cut side down, and bake for 10 to 15 minutes longer, turning the slices midway through, until light golden brown on both sides. Cool completely on the baking sheets on wire racks. Store in airtight containers.

Cornmeal Cookies

These sunny yellow cornmeal hearts bring shortbread to a new taste level; kids and grownups alike won't be able to resist them, so you may want to double the recipe, or use smaller cookie cutters to create more cookies from a single batch.

MAKES 8 COOKIES

1 cup (2 sticks) butter or margarine, softened

½ cup sugar

1 tablespoon vanilla extract

1¼ cups unsifted all-purpose flour

¾ cup yellow cornmeal

Unsalted sunflower seeds

- ◆ Heat the oven to 350°F. Grease 2 baking sheets.

- ◆ In a large bowl, with an electric mixer on medium speed, beat the butter, sugar, and vanilla until fluffy. Add the flour and cornmeal and beat on low speed, scraping the side of bowl occasionally, until well combined.

- ◆ Between lightly floured sheets of waxed paper, roll out the dough to a ¼-inch thickness. With a lightly floured 5-inch heart-shaped cookie cutter, cut out 8 cookie hearts.

- ◆ Place the cookies 1 inch apart on the greased baking sheets. Press the sunflower seeds lightly onto the edges of the cookies and bake for 10 to 12 minutes, or until firm and golden. Cool the cookies on wire racks.

Chocolate Meringue Kisses

These low-fat candylike cookies feature a new ingredient for health-conscious bakers: reduced-fat chocolate-flavor baking chips. Available in supermarkets nationwide, these morsels have less than half the absorbable fat standard chocolate chips have.

MAKES FORTY 1½-INCH COOKIES

3 large egg whites

⅛ teaspoon cream of tartar

¾ cup granulated sugar

⅛ teaspoon salt

3 tablespoons unsweetened cocoa powder

½ cup plus 40 reduced-fat semisweet
      chocolate-flavor baking chips

Confectioners' sugar (optional)

- ◆ Heat the oven to 375°F. Cover 2 large baking sheets with aluminum foil. In a large bowl, with an electric mixer on medium speed, beat the egg whites and cream of tartar until soft peaks form. Gradually add the granulated sugar and salt, beating until the sugar dissolves and very stiff glossy peaks form—about 5 minutes. Sift the cocoa onto the egg-white mixture and gently fold in just until the mixture is blended. Fold in the ½ cup of the chocolate chips.

- ◆ Drop tablespoonfuls of batter, 1 inch apart, onto the prepared sheets. Place 1 of the remaining chocolate chips in the center of each cookie and bake for 30 to 35 minutes, or just until the cookies are dry. Carefully peel the cookies from the foil. Cool completely on wire racks. Sprinkle confectioners' sugar over the cookies, if desired.

Lemon Butter Stars

No July 4th picnic is complete without a constellation of patriotic star-shaped cookies. Pack the cookies in a firm cardboard box or plastic container with waxed paper between each layer. Transfer them to a basket or platter before serving. Decorators' sugar is available at most bakeware shops.

MAKES TEN 6-INCH SUGARED STARS OR FIVE 8-INCH SUGARED STARS

¾ cup granulated sugar

½ cup (1 stick) butter, softened

1 large egg

1 teaspoon lemon extract

1 teaspoon vanilla extract

2 cups unsifted all-purpose flour

½ teaspoon baking powder

¼ teaspoon salt

Red, white, and blue decorator sugar

Confectioners' sugar

Seedless red-raspberry preserves

◆ In a medium-size bowl, with an electric mixer on medium speed, beat the granulated sugar and butter until light and fluffy. Beat in the egg, lemon extract, and vanilla until well mixed. Reduce the mixer speed to low. Gradually beat in the flour, baking powder, and salt. Gather the dough into a ball, flatten it to a 5-inch round, and wrap it in plastic wrap. Refrigerate the dough for at least 30 minutes or overnight.

◆ When the dough has chilled, heat the oven to 325°F. Lightly grease 2 baking sheets. Cut out 2 pieces of waxed paper the same size as the baking sheets. Cut the dough round in half.

◆ Between lightly floured pieces of waxed paper, roll out half of the dough to ¼-inch thickness. Remove the top piece of the waxed paper. With a sharp knife, cut around a 6- or 8-inch star-shaped paper pattern to make as many dough stars as possible, leaving a ½ inch of space between them. Invert the cookies onto a greased baking sheet.

◆ Reroll the dough trimmings between 2 pieces of floured waxed paper to cut out more stars. Repeat with the remaining half of the cookie dough.

◆ Gently place an open 1-inch star-shaped cookie cutter on top of the 6- or 8-inch dough star. Spoon a scant ⅛ teaspoon of the red decorator sugar into the cutter. With a skewer or toothpick, evenly distribute the sugar inside the cutter. Remove the cookie cutter, leaving the red sugar star on the dough. Repeat with the white and blue decorator sugars to make randomly placed stars.

◆ Bake the cookies for 12 to 14 minutes, or until just golden brown at the edges. Cool the cookies for 5 minutes on the baking sheets. Remove the cookies to wire racks and cool them completely.

Chocolate Chunk Cookies

No matter how frequently these all-American treats make their way to dessert tables, they are usually the first to disappear. The mammoth cookies call for great big chocolate chunks, though if you can't find them, regular chocolate chips work just as well. Pile a whole batch in a big napkin-lined basket and send a welcome basket over to new neighbors as a friendly gesture.

MAKES 15 LARGE COOKIES

1 cup (2 sticks) butter or margarine

⅔ cup granulated sugar

½ cup firmly packed light-brown sugar

1 large egg

2 teaspoons vanilla extract

2½ cups unsifted all-purpose flour

½ teaspoon baking soda

¼ teaspoon ground cinnamon

¼ teaspoon salt

1 12-ounce package semisweet chocolate chunks

1 cup walnuts, coarsely chopped

◆ Heat the oven to 375°F. Lightly grease several baking sheets.

◆ In a large bowl, with an electric mixer on medium speed, beat the butter and sugars until light and fluffy. Beat in the egg and vanilla until well combined.

◆ Add the flour, baking soda, cinnamon, and salt. Beat on low speed, scraping side of bowl occasionally, until well combined. Fold in the chocolate chunks and walnuts.

◆ Drop the batter by level ⅓ cupfuls onto the greased baking sheets, leaving plenty of room between the cookies. Pat the cookie dough into ½-inch-thick rounds. Bake for 15 to 20 minutes, or until firm and golden. Cool on wire racks and store in an airtight container.

Linzer Cookies

No need to go to the bakery when you can bake your own nutty, melt-in-your-mouth confections sandwiched with jewel-toned raspberry preserves. Linzer cookies are good travellers, and beloved by picnickers of all ages. Store these in a tin in single layers with a sheet of waxed paper between each layer to save for later or give as gifts.

MAKES 6 COOKIES

½ cup sugar

¾ cup (1½ sticks) butter or margarine, softened

1 large egg

1 teaspoon vanilla extract

1 teaspoon grated lemon rind

2 cups unsifted all-purpose flour

1 cup ground hazelnuts or natural almonds

½ teaspoon salt

½ teaspoon ground cinnamon

⅛ teaspoon ground allspice

9 tablespoons seedless red-raspberry preserves

◆ Set aside 1 tablespoon of the sugar. In a large bowl, with an electric mixer on medium speed, beat the butter and the remaining 7 tablespoons of the sugar until fluffy. Beat in the egg, vanilla, and lemon rind until well combined.

◆ Add the flour, hazelnuts, salt, cinnamon, and allspice. Beat on low speed, scraping the side of bowl occasionally, until well combined. Chill the dough for several hours, or until it is stiff enough to roll.

◆ Divide the dough into thirds. Between sheets of waxed paper, roll out two-thirds of the dough to a ¼-inch thickness. Place the rolled dough in the freezer for 10 minutes to make it more manageable.

◆ Grease 2 baking sheets. With a lightly floured 6-inch scalloped heart-shaped cookie cutter, or a 6-inch heart-shaped paper pattern and fluted pastry cutter, cut out 6 cookie hearts from the rolled dough, reserving the scraps. Place the hearts, about 1 inch apart, on the greased baking sheets. Spread 1½ tablespoons of the raspberry preserves onto each cookie heart.

◆ Roll out the remaining dough with the reserved scraps to make a 12- by 9-inch rectangle. Place the dough in the freezer for 10 minutes to make it more manageable.

◆ Heat the oven to 375°F. With a fluted pastry cutter, cut the rectangle lengthwise into 18 strips. Then cut the strips in half crosswise to make thirty-six 6- by ½-inch strips. On each cookie, place 3 strips evenly spaced across the top of the preserves in one direction and 3 strips in the opposite direction to form a lattice effect. Trim off the excess pastry-strip ends. Sprinkle some of the remaining 1 tablespoon sugar onto the lattice design on each cookie.

◆ Bake the cookies for 16 to 18 minutes, or until firm and golden. Cool on wire racks and store the cookies in an airtight container.

Spiral & Zebra Cookies

Chocolate-and-vanilla icebox cookies are pure nostalgia. They can be fashioned into several decorative designs. The dough should be refrigerated for at least two hours or up to several days before using, and can be frozen up to four months if tightly wrapped.

MAKES 6 LARGE SPIRAL OR 8 ZEBRA COOKIES

1 cup (2 sticks) butter or margarine, softened

¾ cup sugar

1 large egg

1 tablespoon vanilla extract

2½ cups unsifted all-purpose flour

½ teaspoon baking powder

½ teaspoon salt

2 1-ounce squares unsweetened chocolate, melted

◆ In a medium-size bowl, with an electric mixer on medium speed, beat together the butter, sugar, egg, and vanilla until fluffy. Stir in the flour, baking powder, and salt until well combined.

◆ Divide the dough in half. Wrap 1 dough half in plastic wrap. Stir the chocolate into the remaining half of the dough and then wrap in plastic wrap. Set both doughs aside at room temperature for 30 minutes.

LARGE SPIRAL COOKIES

◆ Between sheets of waxed paper, roll out each dough separately to make 16- by 4-inch rectangles. Brush the surface of the chocolate dough with water. Place the other dough on top and brush the surface with water. From the 4-inch edge, roll up the dough tightly, jelly-roll fashion.

Stand the roll on one end and gently press down to make a 4-inch-diameter roll. Wrap the dough in plastic wrap and refrigerate for 30 minutes.

◆ Heat the oven to 375°F. Grease several baking sheets. Slice the roll crosswise into six ½-inch-wide rounds. Place the rounds, 2 inches apart, among the greased baking sheets. Bake for 10 to 12 minutes, or until lightly browned and firm. Cool the cookies completely on wire racks and store in an airtight container.

ZEBRA COOKIES

◆ Between sheets of waxed paper, roll out each dough separately to an 8-inch square. Brush the surface of the chocolate dough with water. Place the other dough on top and brush the surface with water. Cut the double-layer dough stack into quarters. Brush the surface of each quarter with water. Stack one on top of the other with the colors alternating. Wrap the dough in plastic wrap and refrigerate.

◆ Heat the oven to 375°F. Grease several baking sheets. Slice the dough crosswise into eight ½-inch-wide rounds. Place the rectangles, 2 inches apart, among the greased baking sheets. Bake for 10 to 12 minutes, or until lightly browned and firm. Cool the cookies completely on wire racks and then store in an airtight container.

LIGHTING THE SCENE

A well-lit picnic or porch supper creates an unforgettable ambiance. Hurricane lamps furnished with votive or pillar candles cast a flickering glow and since the glass protects the flame from blowing out, they are preferable when it's breezy outside. Oil lamps or lanterns provide a stronger, steadier light, and can be used for either occasion. Chinese lanterns also provide steady, muted light and can easily be strung on a porch for evening affairs.

Craft your own luminarias using paper bags. Simply cut out small, decorative designs along the top third of a paper lunch bag, fill the bag with three to four inches of sand, and nestle a votive candle inside. Line them up along a path leading to the porch, or set them around the outermost perimeters of your picnic area.

Moravian star pointed spheres, in which you burn votives, are handsome strung up from porch ceilings or hanging from tree limbs.

You can always create natural candle holders with fruit by carving a hole in the top of an apple large enough to snugly fit a taper candle or make a well in the top of an orange deep enough to set in a votive, surround the edge of the candle with cloves pushed all the way

in to form a decorative border; cut enough pineapple flesh out of the whole fruit to sink in a pillar candle, or scoop out all the flesh and carve a face or a circle of small triangles for light to pass through the skin. Place a votive inside to create a summertime version of a jack o'lantern.

Creme de Menthe Brownies

Want a triple decker of fudgy brownies, minty icing, and chocolate topping to become a part of your dessert repertoire? These gooey treats far surpass the most illustrious of gourmet-shop offerings. Pile them on a plate garnished with fresh sprigs of mint for your dessert table, or wrap the refrigerated bars in aluminum foil for picnics.

MAKES 18 SERVINGS

Chocolate Base

½ cup (1 stick) butter or margarine, softened

1 cup granulated sugar

4 large eggs

1 cup unsifted all-purpose flour

½ teaspoon salt

1 16-ounce can chocolate-flavored syrup

1 teaspoon vanilla extract

Mint Icing

¼ cup (½ stick) butter or margarine, softened

2 cups confectioners' sugar

2 tablespoons mint-flavored liqueur

Sweet Chocolate Topping

1 12-ounce package semisweet chocolate chips

½ cup (1 stick) butter or margarine

♦ Prepare the chocolate base: Heat the oven to 350°F. Grease and lightly flour a 13- by 9-inch baking pan. In a large bowl, with an electric mixer on medium speed, beat the butter until light and fluffy. Gradually beat in the granulated sugar until well combined. Add the eggs, 1 at a time, beating well after each addition.

♦ In a small bowl or on a sheet of waxed paper, combine the flour and salt. Beat the flour mixture, chocolate syrup, and vanilla into the butter mixture until well combined. Pour the batter into the prepared baking pan. Bake for 25 to 30 minutes, or until a cake tester comes out clean when inserted in the center. Cool the base completely in the pan on a wire rack.

♦ Prepare the mint icing: In a medium-size bowl, beat the butter until light and fluffy. Gradually beat in the confectioners' sugar and liqueur until the mixture is smooth. Spread the icing evenly over the top of the cooled chocolate base in the baking pan. Refrigerate for at least 1 hour, or until well chilled.

♦ Prepare the sweet chocolate topping: In the top of a double boiler or a heatproof bowl over simmering water, stir the chocolate chips and butter together until the mixture is melted and smooth. Spread the topping evenly over the icing in the baking pan. Cover and refrigerate for at least 1 hour, or until set. Cut the brownies into bars to serve. Cover and refrigerate any leftovers.

Coconut-Pecan Squares

This light vanilla sheet cake is topped with coconut-pecan frosting that's passed under the broiler for a toasty finishing touch. To present the cake after a porch supper, garnish the platter with some fresh ripe strawberries for a bit of color.

MAKES 9 SERVINGS

Vanilla Cake

1³⁄₄ cups unsifted all-purpose flour

³⁄₄ cup granulated sugar

2 teaspoons baking powder

¹⁄₄ teaspoon salt

²⁄₃ cup milk

¹⁄₃ cup vegetable oil

1 large egg

2 teaspoons vanilla extract

Coconut-Pecan Frosting

1 cup pecan halves

¹⁄₂ cup flaked coconut

¹⁄₂ cup firmly packed light-brown sugar

¹⁄₃ cup heavy cream

1 teaspoon vanilla extract

¹⁄₄ teaspoon salt

2 tablespoons dried sour cherries (optional)

◆ Prepare the cake: Heat the oven to 350°F. Grease a 9-inch square baking pan.

◆ Into a medium-size bowl, measure the flour, granulated sugar, baking powder, and salt. Add the milk, oil, egg, and vanilla. With an electric mixer on medium speed, beat the mixture, scraping the side of the bowl occasionally with a rubber spatula, until a smooth batter forms. Spread the batter evenly in the greased pan.

◆ Bake for 25 to 30 minutes, or until a cake tester inserted in the center comes out clean. Remove the cake from the oven and heat the broiler.

◆ Prepare the coconut-pecan frosting: In a medium-size bowl, with a fork, stir the pecans, coconut, brown sugar, cream, vanilla, and salt until the mixture is well combined.

◆ Spread the coconut-pecan frosting evenly over the top of the cake. Transfer to the broiler and broil 6 inches from the heat source for 2 to 3 minutes—just until it bubbles and the tips of the coconut brown slightly. Remove the cake to a wire rack and sprinkle with the dried cherries, if desired, and cool until ready to serve. Cut the cake into 9 squares, transfer the squares to a serving plate, and serve.

Peach-Berry Cobbler

A fitting finale to any summer porch supper, cobbler featuring ripe summer fruit is best served warm from the oven with a dollop of whipped cream (or for those wishing to gild the lily, with a scoop of vanilla ice cream). Gooseberries provide a tart counterpart to sweet summer peaches and strawberries in this sumptuous cobbler.

MAKES 8 SERVINGS

Peach-Berry Filling

6 medium-size ripe fresh peaches, peeled, halved,
    pitted, and sliced

3 cups (1½ pints) fresh strawberries, quartered

1 cup (½ pint) gooseberries

2 tablespoons granulated sugar

Cornmeal-Cobbler Topping

¾ cup unsifted all-purpose flour

½ cup yellow cornmeal

3 tablespoons granulated sugar

2 teaspoons baking powder

⅛ teaspoon salt

6 tablespoons (¾ stick) butter

5 tablespoons milk

Whipped Cream (optional)

½ cup heavy cream

1 teaspoon confectioners' sugar

◆ Prepare the peach-berry filling: Lightly grease an 8-inch square by 2-inch-deep baking dish. In a medium-size bowl, combine the peaches, strawberries, gooseberries, and granulated sugar. Pour the peach-berry filling into the greased baking dish and set aside.

◆ Prepare the cornmeal-cobbler topping: Heat the oven to 375°F. In a medium-size bowl, combine the flour, cornmeal, 2 tablespoons of the granulated sugar, the baking powder, and salt. With a pastry blender or 2 knives, cut in the butter until the mixture resembles coarse crumbs. Sprinkle in the milk, 1 tablespoon at a time, mixing lightly with a fork until a loose dough forms. Gather the dough into a ball. On a lightly floured surface, knead the dough 8 to 10 times, or until it is fairly smooth.

◆ On a lightly floured surface, roll the dough out to an 8-inch square. Place the dough on top of the filling. With a knife, randomly cut holes in the dough to allow the steam to escape.

◆ Bake the cobbler for 30 to 35 minutes, or until the topping is golden brown and the juices bubble in the center. Cool on a wire rack for 10 minutes. Sprinkle with the remaining 1 tablespoon sugar.

◆ Meanwhile, prepare the whipped cream, if desired: In a small bowl, with an electric mixer on medium speed, beat the heavy cream with the confectioners' sugar until stiff peaks form when the beaters are lifted.

◆ Spoon the cobbler onto serving plates and serve with the whipped cream.

Rose-Scented Geranium Cake

Edible rose geranium leaves perfume this batter with a beguiling floral essence. To make the vanilla sugar, bury a split-open vanilla bean in a jar of superfine sugar and let sit for a few days before using. Top the jar with fresh sugar as you use it as the pod will continue flavoring the sugar for several months. Baking the cake in a fluted pan creates a festive shape perfect for tea parties. Serve the cake on its own, or garnish it with fresh berries. If you are traveling with the cake, tightly wrap it in plastic wrap and slice it just before serving.

MAKES 4 TO 6 SERVINGS

The weight of the unshelled eggs in:

Butter

Vanilla-flavored sugar

1 teaspoon rose water

2 large eggs

All-purpose flour, sifted

A little confectioners' sugar

4 or 5 rose geranium leaves

◆ Heat the oven to 350°F. In a large bowl, with an electric mixer on medium speed, cream the butter with the sugar and the rose water until light and fluffy. Beat in the eggs, 1 at a time, making sure that the mixture does not separate. Carefully fold in the sifted flour.

◆ Butter an 8-inch round baking pan and line the base with a round of buttered waxed paper. Sprinkle a thin layer of the sugar over the inside of the cake pan. Lay the leaves upside down in the base of the pan. Carefully spoon the mixture on top, taking care not to dislodge the leaves.

◆ Bake the cake for 25 to 35 minutes, or until a toothpick inserted in the center comes out clean and the cake springs back when lightly pressed with a fingertip. Take care not to overbake the cake. Remove from the oven and cool in the pan for 3 minutes, then turn out on to a wire rack. Remove the waxed paper and dust a little sifted confectioners' sugar around the edge of the cake. Cool the cake completely and serve.

Raspberry & Fig Tart

The sublime flavor of fresh figs plays off the tang of red raspberries in this sophisticated tart. This dish does not travel well, so if you plan on an outdoor affair, make the tart as close to the time you are leaving as possible to avoid the crust becoming soggy.

MAKES 8 SERVINGS

Almond Pastry

1 cup unsifted all-purpose flour

½ cup ground natural almonds

2 tablespoons sugar

¼ teaspoon salt

½ cup (1 stick) butter, cut in small pieces

1 teaspoon almond extract

2 to 4 tablespoons ice water

Raspberry-Fig Filling

⅓ cup seedless red-raspberry preserves

2 tablespoons fresh lemon juice

6 large (about 8 ounces) fresh figs

1 cup (½ pint) fresh red raspberries

Fresh mint sprig (optional)

◆ Prepare the almond pastry: In a medium-size bowl, combine the flour, almonds, sugar, and salt. With a pastry blender or 2 knives, cut the butter into the flour mixture until the mixture resembles coarse crumbs. Sprinkle in the almond extract and then the water, 1 tablespoon at a time, mixing lightly with a fork until the pastry is moist enough to hold together when lightly pressed. Shape the pastry into a flat ball. Wrap the pastry in plastic wrap and refrigerate for 30 minutes.

◆ When the pastry has chilled, heat the oven to 375°F. Between 2 sheets of floured waxed paper, roll out the pastry to a 12-inch round. Remove the top sheet of waxed paper and invert the pastry into a 9½-inch tart pan with a removable bottom, allowing the excess to extend over the edge. Remove the remaining sheet of waxed paper. Fold the excess pastry inside so that it is even around the top edge with the rim of the pan. Press the pastry against the side to make an even thickness. With a fork, pierce the bottom of the pastry crust to prevent shrinkage. Line the crust with a piece of aluminum foil, allowing the foil to extend over the edge of the crust, and fill with uncooked dried beans or pie weights.

◆ Bake the pastry crust for 10 minutes. Remove from the oven and remove the foil with the beans and bake the crust for another 12 to 15 minutes longer, or until crisp and golden. Cool completely on a wire rack.

◆ No more than 1 hour before serving, prepare the raspberry-fig filling: In a small bowl, combine the preserves and lemon juice; set aside. Cut the figs lengthwise in half. With a pastry brush, spread 2 tablespoons of the preserve mixture evenly over the bottom of the crust. Arrange 8 fig halves, cut sides up with the stems toward the center, around the edge of the crust. Place the remaining 4 fig halves in the center with the stems pointed out.

◆ Place 3 large berries in the center of the tart. Arrange the remaining berries in the spaces between the figs. Brush the remaining preserve mixture over the figs and berries.

◆ Remove the rim of the pan from the tart. Place the tart on a serving plate. Top with the mint sprig, if desired.

Bourbon Carrot Cake

Brimming with aromatic spices and blanketed in rich cream cheese frosting, this moist, dense dessert will convert even the staunchest non-believer into a carrot cake lover. A garnish of bourbon-soaked carrot shreds and ground walnuts rivals the presentation of a professional bakery cake, right from your own kitchen!

MAKES 16 SERVINGS

¾ cup golden raisins

½ cup bourbon

2 cups unsifted all-purpose flour

2 teaspoons baking soda

2 teaspoons ground cinnamon

1 teaspoon salt

1 teaspoon ground nutmeg

½ teaspoon ground allspice

½ teaspoon ground cloves

1½ cups vegetable oil

1⅓ cups granulated sugar

½ cup firmly packed light-brown sugar

4 large eggs

8 medium-size carrots, peeled and coarsely shredded
(about 4½ cups)

1 cup plus 3 tablespoons ground walnuts

½ cup (1 stick) butter, softened

1 8-ounce package cream cheese

1 teaspoon vanilla extract

1 1-pound package (3½ cups) confectioners' sugar

◆ In a small bowl, combine the raisins and bourbon. Set the mixture aside for 1 hour to soak.

◆ Heat the oven to 350°F. Grease and flour two 9-inch round baking pans. In a medium-size bowl, combine the flour, baking soda, cinnamon, salt, nutmeg, allspice, and cloves.

◆ In a large bowl, with an electric mixer on medium speed, beat the oil, granulated sugar, brown sugar, and eggs until well combined, scraping the side of the bowl occasionally with a rubber spatula. Reduce the speed to low and beat in the flour mixture just until combined. Drain the raisins, reserving the bourbon, and fold in 3 cups of the carrots, the raisins, and 1 cup of the walnuts. Divide the batter evenly between the prepared pans.

◆ Bake the cakes for 35 to 40 minutes, or until a cake tester inserted in the center comes out clean. Cool in the pans on wire racks for 10 minutes. Invert the cakes onto the racks and remove the pans. Cool completely.

◆ In a small saucepan, combine the reserved bourbon and the remaining 1½ cups carrots. Cook over high heat for 2 to 3 minutes, or just until the carrots soften and most of the bourbon evaporates. Set aside to cool completely.

◆ In a large bowl, with an electric mixer on medium speed, beat the butter and cream cheese until smooth. Beat in the vanilla and slowly beat in the confectioners' sugar.

◆ Place 1 cake layer on a serving plate and spread one-third of the frosting over the top. Place another cake layer evenly on the frosted layer. Frost the side and top of the cake with the remaining frosting. Sprinkle the bourbon-carrot shreds on the top and side of the frosted cake. Sprinkle the remaining 3 tablespoons of the walnuts around the bottom edge of the cake to form a border. Refrigerate until ready to serve.

Pumpkin-Pecan Pie

Why not serve two favorites in a single pie for autumn suppers and tailgate picnics. Guests will be surprised to find a creamy pumpkin filling beneath what appears to be a traditional pecan pie. This pie is so rich, small slices will satisfy the most indulgent sweet tooth.

MAKES 12 TO 14 SERVINGS

Butter Crust

¾ cup (1½ sticks) butter or margarine

2 cups unsifted all-purpose flour

6 to 7 tablespoons cold water

Pumpkin Layer

2 large eggs, separated

½ cup sugar

1 16-ounce can pumpkin, or 2 cups well-drained
    fresh pumpkin puree

½ cup half-and-half

2 teaspoons pumpkin-pie spice

½ teaspoon salt

Pecan Layer

3 tablespoons butter or margarine

½ cup sugar

1 cup dark corn syrup

1 teaspoon vanilla extract

2 large eggs

2 cups pecan halves

◆ Prepare the butter crust: In a large bowl, with a pastry blender or 2 knives, cut the butter into the flour until the mixture resembles coarse crumbs. Sprinkle in the cold water, one tablespoon at a time, mixing lightly after each addition, just until the pastry holds together. Divide the pastry in half and shape each half into a disk. Wrap each disk in plastic wrap and refrigerate for at least 1 hour.

◆ On a lightly floured surface, with a floured rolling pin, roll the pastry into a 12-inch round. Line a 9-inch pie plate with the pastry, fold the overhang under, and form a high fluted edge. Repeat with the other half of the pastry and refrigerate.

◆ Preheat the oven to 350°F. Prepare the pumpkin layer: In a small bowl, with an electric mixer on high speed, beat the egg whites until soft peaks form. Gradually beat in the sugar until stiff, glossy peaks form. In a large bowl, with the same beaters and the mixer on low speed, beat the egg yolks, pumpkin, half-and-half, pumpkin spice, and salt until blended. With a rubber spatula, fold the egg whites into the pumpkin mixture. Pour into the pie shells and bake for 30 minutes.

◆ Prepare the pecan layer: In a 1-quart saucepan over low heat, melt the butter. Remove from the heat and stir in the sugar, corn syrup, and vanilla until blended. Beat in the eggs.

◆ Carefully arrange the pecans in a single layer over the pumpkin layer in a circular pattern. Pour the sugar mixture over the pecans, being careful not to disturb them.

◆ Bake the pies until a knife inserted 1 inch from the edge comes out clean—15 to 20 minutes longer. Cool the pies completely on wire racks. Gently cover and refrigerate until serving time. For picnics, wrap the pies in plastic wrap and stow in the cooler.

Colonial Apple Pie

Supper guests will be transported back to the good old days with apple pie served with a scoop of vanilla ice cream or a wedge of Cheddar cheese. If you are taking this pie along on picnics, make sure to wrap it all around from the bottom so none of the juice escapes while it's being toted. Nestle the pie snugly in a pie carrier to keep it from sliding around.

MAKES 8 SERVINGS

1½ cups unsifted all-purpose flour

½ cup plus 2 tablespoons sugar

½ cup (1 stick) butter or margarine

2 large eggs

Cold water

1 teaspoon ground cinnamon

Vanilla wafer cookies

7 Golden Delicious or green cooking apples

½ cup dried currants

2 tablespoons apple jelly

◆ In a medium-size bowl, combine the flour and 2 tablespoons of the sugar. With a pastry blender or 2 knives, cut in the butter until the mixture resembles coarse crumbs. Beat the eggs in a 1-cup measuring cup. Add enough cold water to measure ⅔ cup. Add about 5 tablespoons of the egg mixture, 1 tablespoon at a time, to the flour mixture, mixing lightly with a fork until the pastry holds together. Gather the pastry into a ball.

◆ On a lightly floured surface, with a floured rolling pin, roll the pastry into a 14-inch round. Carefully lift the pastry onto a large baking sheet. Chill the pastry.

◆ In a small bowl, combine the remaining ½ cup sugar and the cinnamon. Crush enough wafers to make ½ cup crumbs. Peel, core, and thinly slice 5 of the apples.

◆ Heat the oven to 400°F. Remove the pastry round from the refrigerator. Fold ½ inch of the pastry toward the center along the edge to form a double-thick edge. Brush the pastry with some of the reserved egg mixture. Sprinkle the center of the pastry with half of the wafer crumbs to form a 9-inch round. Arrange half of the apple slices in an even layer over the crumbs. Sprinkle with half of the cinnamon sugar and currants.

◆ Arrange the remaining half of the apple slices on top to form a neat, compact, even mound of apples about 9 inches in diameter and 2 inches high. It should look like a baking pan sitting in the middle of the pastry. Sprinkle the apples with the remaining half of the crumbs, the cinnamon sugar, and currants.

◆ Peel, core, and thinly slice the remaining 2 apples. Arrange on top of the crumb mixture in an attractive pattern around the edge and in the center. Bring the pastry up all around and over the mound of apples to form an open "bag." The pastry will naturally form gathers or pleats; press the pastry firmly on the top to keep the pastry from opening during baking. Brush the pastry edge with the remaining egg mixture. Cover the center of the pie with a round of aluminum foil.

◆ Bake the pie for 25 minutes. Lower the oven temperature to 350°F and continue to bake until the apples are tender—about 20 minutes. If the pastry browns too much, cover with strips of aluminum foil. Remove the foil from the center 5 minutes before the pie is done.

◆ Cool the pie completely. Melt the apple jelly in a small saucepan, and brush over the top apple slices and pastry.

Wild-Strawberry Pudding

For picnics, refrigerate the entire batch of pudding in a tightly lidded plastic container and transport in a cooler; spoon individual servings into pretty paper cups and garnish with strawberries carried separately.

MAKES 4 SERVINGS

⅓ cup sugar

3 tablespoons cornstarch

⅛ teaspoon salt

2 cups milk

1 cup wild strawberries

1 large egg, lightly beaten

2 teaspoons strawberry-flavored liqueur or brandy

Small strawberries and blossoms (optional)

◆ In the top of a double boiler, mix the sugar, cornstarch, and salt. Gradually stir in the milk. Place over boiling water and cook, stirring constantly, for 6 to 8 minutes, or until the mixture thickens to a pudding consistency. Cover and cook over simmering water for 5 minutes longer, stirring occasionally.

◆ Meanwhile, in a food processor fitted with the chopping blade or a blender, puree the wild strawberries. Strain through a fine strainer; discard the seeds and pulp.

◆ In small bowl, gradually beat half of the hot pudding mixture into the egg. Beat the egg mixture back into the pudding mixture in the double boiler and cook, stirring constantly, for 2 minutes. Remove the pudding from the heat and stir in the liqueur and strawberry puree. Divide the pudding mixture among 4 stemmed glasses and cool to room temperature. Cover and refrigerate for several hours, or until firm. Garnish the puddings with strawberries and blossoms, if desired.

Mixed-Berry Bread Pudding

One of the classic summer treats, bread pudding melts in your mouth when served slightly warm, though you can transport it tightly wrapped in foil to picnics and slice when it's time for dessert.

MAKES 8 SERVINGS

8 slices firm white bread, cut into ½-inch cubes

2 cups fresh strawberries, quartered

1 cup each fresh blueberries and raspberries

⅓ cup granulated sugar

2 large eggs

2 tablespoons butter, melted

2 teaspoons ground cinnamon

2 teaspoons vanilla extract

1½ cups half-and-half

Confectioners' sugar (optional)

- Generously grease a 9- by 5-inch loaf pan and place in a baking pan to catch any drips.

- Heat the oven to 350°F. In a large bowl, combine the bread cubes, strawberries, blueberries, and raspberries. Transfer the bread mixture to the greased pan. In a 4-cup measuring cup, beat the granulated sugar, eggs, butter, cinnamon, and vanilla until smooth. Gradually beat in the half-and-half. Pour over the bread mixture.

- Bake for 30 minutes, or until the top is golden. Cover with aluminum foil and bake for 30 minutes longer, or until a knife inserted in the center comes out clean. Cool the pudding completely in the pan on a wire rack.

- To serve, cut the pudding crosswise into 8 slices. Place each slice on a serving plate. Sprinkle the tops of the pudding slices with confectioners' sugar.

The Best Rice Pudding

When Country Living's food editor Joanne Lamb Hayes and co-author Bonnie Tandy Leblang created this recipe for their book Rice (Harmony), *their main requirement was that the result taste just like Mom's. This version of the old-time favorite has all the nostalgic flavor you may remember.*

MAKES 4 SERVINGS

1 cup water

½ cup short- or medium-grain white rice

½ vanilla bean, split

¼ teaspoon salt

2 cups milk

1 cup (½ pint) heavy cream

½ cup sugar

2 large eggs

½ cup dark seedless raisins or dried sour cherries

¼ teaspoon ground cinnamon

Boiling water

- In a 2-quart saucepan, heat water to boiling. Add the rice, vanilla bean, and salt. Cook for 10 minutes.

- Add the milk and cook over very low heat until the rice is tender—about 10 minutes.

- Preheat the oven to 350°F. Lightly butter a 1½-quart shallow baking dish.

- In a small bowl, combine the cream, sugar, and eggs. Fold into the rice mixture along with the raisins. Remove the vanilla bean and pour the rice mixture into the buttered baking dish. Sprinkle the top of the mixture evenly with the cinnamon.

- Place the baking dish into a large baking pan in the oven. Pour the boiling water into the baking pan to a depth of 1 inch. Bake for 30 to 45 minutes, or until the pudding is firm and the top surface is golden brown. Cool to room temperature on a wire rack and serve.

BEVERAGES

Out in the fresh air, everyone works up a real thirst. Offer up plenty of cool quenchers over a shower of ice on hot summer days; keep an ice-filled tub or cooler well stocked when weather is balmy so beverages stay frosty cold. On brisk days have a thermosful of steaming hot drinks ready to warm the hands and hearts of your guests.

Hot Spiced Tea

Tea steeped with orange peel and cloves is an aromatic beverage that can be served hot, or refrigerated and poured over ice on warm days. The honey can be omitted, or increased according to taste. For a special touch, add a cinnamon stick and thin slices of orange and apple to each cup.

MAKES 1 SERVING

2 whole cloves

1 3-inch strip orange peel

Cold water

1 tea bag

½ teaspoon honey

◆ Insert the cloves into the orange peel. Fill a microwave-safe cup with the cold water to within ½-inch of the top of the cup and add the clove-studded orange peel. Microwave, uncovered, on high (100 percent) for 1½ to 2 minutes, or until the water is steaming.

◆ Add the tea bag and honey to the water mixture and microwave on high (100 percent) for 30 seconds. Allow the tea to steep; cool slightly. Remove the tea bag and serve.

Iced Mint Tea

Nothing cools off a crowd on a hot summer day better than tall glasses of frosty iced tea embellished with fresh sprigs of mint. Refrigerate the steeped tea until cold before pouring into an insulated thermos jug with ice; the cubes should last for several hours. Wrap the mint sprigs loosely in a damp paper towel and stow in a plastic bag until just before serving.

MAKES 12 SERVINGS

8 mint-flavored tea bags

8 cups boiling water

Sugar (optional)

8 cups ice cubes

Fresh mint sprigs

◆ In a heat-proof container, combine the tea bags and boiling water. Let the mixture steep for 30 minutes. Remove the tea bags and stir in the sugar to taste, if desired, and 4 cups of the ice cubes. Pour the tea into a large jar or pitcher and garnish with the mint sprigs. To serve, pour the tea into glasses over the remaining 4 cups of ice cubes.

Basic Hot Chocolate

Once you realize how easy and economical it is to fix the richest, creamiest hot chocolate you've ever tasted, you'll never go back to the store-bought variety. Adjust the amount of sugar and cocoa to suit your preferences (though remember unsweetened cocoa powder is intensely chocolatey). This drink can be prepared in a saucepan over medium heat if you don't have a microwave. Gussy up a basic cup with marshmallows, whipped cream, a sprinkle of cinnamon or cocoa powder, a cinnamon stick or candy cane stirrer.

MAKES 1 SERVING

1 cup skim milk

2 teaspoons sugar

1 teaspoon unsweetened cocoa powder

Miniature marshmallows (optional)

◆ In a microwave-safe cup, beat the milk, sugar, and cocoa until well combined. Microwave on high (100 percent) for 2 to 2½ minutes, or until the mixture is heated through. Stir again and serve immediately. Top with marshmallows, if desired.

BEVERAGE SERVICE

For porch suppers, keep bottled water, and bottles or cans of juice, soda, and beer icy cold by filling a large galvanized metal tub or wheelbarrow with ice and submerging the drinks; keep the tub in a shady spot so guests can help themselves. On picnics, fill an insulated cooler with ice to submerge drinks. A small gathering may require nothing more than cool water; carry plastic bottles of spring water that have been frozen solid . . . by the time you reach your destination, the ice should be melted back into water and still cold and refreshing. Put out a pitcher of water next to some glasses and a bucket of ice. A bowl of sliced lemons, limes, and oranges and some fresh mint sprigs are a lovely garnish.

Grape Tea Punch

Herbal tea blended with white grapes becomes a subtly flavored, rosy-hued punch that can be topped off with Champagne or ginger ale for a sophisticated cocktail. Pack the Champagne or ginger ale separately and combine just prior to serving.

MAKES 24 SERVINGS

2 quarts boiling water

8 bags red herbal tea

2 24-ounce bottles unsweetened white grape juice

Ice cubes

Fresh strawberries, rinsed and dried

Champagne or Chilled ginger ale

◆ In a 5-quart heatproof container or bowl, combine the water and tea bags. Cool the tea mixture, stirring occasionally, to room temperature. Remove and discard the tea bags. Add the grape juice to the tea. Cover and refrigerate until ready to serve.

◆ To serve, place some of the ice cubes in a 4- to 6-quart punch bowl. Pour the punch over the ice and add the strawberries to the punch bowl. Ladle some of the punch base into glasses to fill half way. Add the Champagne or ginger ale, as your guests desire, to fill the glasses completely. Gently stir to combine.

Pineapple Punch

If you are preparing this punch ahead, make sure to stir it before serving. Festive garnishes include pineapple wedges perched on the edge of the glass, a sprinkle of grated fresh coconut, or even corny but fun paper umbrellas.

MAKES 3 SERVINGS

Milk from 1 coconut

2 cups fresh pineapple chunks

1 12-ounce can guanabana (soursop) juice

1 cup ice cubes

◆ Pour the coconut milk into the container of a blender. Add the pineapple chunks, guanabana juice, and ice cubes to the blender. Blend until the mixture is smooth. Serve immediately or refrigerate until ready to serve.

Carambola Cooler

Otherwise known as starfruit, tart yellow carambola forms celestial shapes when sliced crosswise. Freezing the slices before adding them to the punch serves double duty by keeping the drink cool without watering down the flavor with melting ice, a real plus when transporting in a thermos to picnics. This star-spangled cooler is the drink to pour on July 4th; add a shot of vodka or rum per serving for an alcoholic version.

MAKES 6 SERVINGS

1 medium-size carambola

6 cups water

½ cup sugar

½ cup fresh lime juice

3 tablespoons grenadine syrup

◆ Cut the carambola crosswise into ¼-inch-thick slices. Place the slices on a piece of waxed paper or baking sheet.

Freeze the carambola slices until solid—about 2 hours.

◆ In a 2-quart saucepan, heat the water and sugar to boiling. Remove from the heat and stir in the lime juice and grenadine syrup. Strain the mixture through a fine strainer or a cheesecloth. Refrigerate until well chilled.

◆ To serve, pour the chilled cooler into glasses and float the frozen carambola slices on top. Serve immediately.

Polynesian Yogurt Shake

Try this puree of sweet papaya and banana with yogurt and honey as a healthful breakfast shake or as a quick-to-prepare refresher on a hot afternoon. For a splash of color, adorn the rim of each glass with a ripe strawberry.

MAKES 3 SERVINGS

1 large papaya

2 very ripe bananas

½ cup plain yogurt

1 tablespoon fresh lemon juice

1 tablespoon honey

2 cups ice cubes

◆ Peel, seed, and cube the papaya. Peel and cut the bananas into large chunks. In a blender, puree the papaya, banana, yogurt, lemon juice, and honey until smooth. Add the ice cubes and blend until smooth.

◆ To serve, pour the shake into glasses and serve immediately or refrigerate until ready to serve.

Red-Hot Bloody Mary

While this revved-up version of the traditional brunch beverage is already super spicy, you can turn up the heat even more by increasing the amount of hot pepper sauce and horseradish used here.

MAKES 6 SERVINGS

3 cups tomato juice

6 ounces (¾ cup) pepper or plain vodka

3 tablespoons prepared horseradish

3 tablespoons lemon juice

2 tablespoons Worcestershire sauce

½ teaspoon hot red-pepper sauce

½ teaspoon ground black pepper

Ice cubes

6 small celery sticks

◆ In a 2-quart pitcher, combine the tomato juice, vodka, horseradish, lemon juice, Worcestershire, red-pepper sauce, and black pepper.

◆ To serve, fill 6 glasses with ice cubes. Divide the tomato mixture among the glasses. Garnish each glass with a celery stick.

Margaritas

For a frozen version, mix the margaritas in a blender until the ice becomes slush.

MAKES 2 SERVINGS

½ cup fresh lime juice

Coarse (kosher) salt (optional)

1 cup ice

½ cup orange-flavored liqueur

¼ cup tequila

◆ If salted glass rims are desired, with a pastry brush, moisten the rim of 2 large, shallow cocktail glasses with some of the lime juice. Coat the glass rims with salt.

◆ In a 1-quart container with a tight fitting lid, shake together the ice, lime juice, orange-flavored liqueur, and tequila. Strain the Margaritas into prepared glasses and discard the ice. Serve immediately or pack in a thermos.

Frozen Honeydew Margaritas

This can be served without the alcohol—use three tablespoons of sugar instead of just one.

MAKES 4 SERVINGS

1 1-pound wedge honeydew melon, seeded

½ cup fresh lime juice

Coarse (kosher) salt (optional)

¼ cup orange-flavored liqueur or
    orange juice

¼ cup tequila or orange juice

1 or 3 tablespoons sugar

4 lime slices

◆ Several hours or the day before serving, prepare the honeydew for freezing: Peel the honeydew and cut into 1-inch cubes. Arrange the cubes in a single layer in an aluminum-foil-lined 13- by 9-inch baking pan. Cover tightly and freeze.

◆ Just before serving, if salted glass rims are desired, with a pastry brush, moisten the rims of 4 large, shallow cocktail glasses with some of the lime juice. Coat the glass rims with salt.

◆ In a a food processor fitted with the chopping blade, blend the frozen melon cubes, remaining lime juice, the orange-flavored liqueur, tequila, and sugar until the melon is pureed. Divide the mixture among the prepared glasses. Insert one lime slice into each glass, if desired.

Fresh Juice Blend

Sweet, ripe mangoes balance out the tartness of grapefruit and add body to this sublime breakfast drink.

MAKES 4 SERVINGS

5 to 6 pink grapefruits, halved

1 mango, peeled, pitted and cut into chunks

1 tablespoon honey

1 cup ice cubes (optional)

◆ With a juicer, squeeze the grapefruits to get 3½ cups of juice. Set the juice aside.

◆ In a blender, puree the mango with the honey until the mixture is smooth. Add the mango mixture to the grapefruit juice and stir well. Strain the juice blend and chill for at least 1 hour. Serve over ice, if desired.

California Lemonade

Chardonnay or other light white wine give this refreshing lemonade a kick.

MAKES 12 SERVINGS

2 lemons, thinly sliced

1 lime, thinly sliced

⅓ cup sugar

1 750-milliliter bottle white wine

5 cups ice cubes

◆ In 2½-quart pitcher or container, combine the lemon and lime slices with the sugar. With a wooden spoon, press the slices to extract some of the juice and to dissolve the sugar. Stir in the wine and ice cubes. To serve, pour into stemmed glasses.

Index

Photography Credits